NEW STUDIES IN BIBLICAL THEOLOGY

D. A. Carson, Series Editor

NEW STUDIES IN BIBLICAL THEOLOGY

Possessed by God
DAVID PETERSON

Whoredom
RAYMOND C. ORTLUND, JR.

Jesus and the Logic of History
PAUL W. BARNETT

Hear, My Son
DANIEL J. ESTES

Hear, My Son

Teaching and Learning in Proverbs 1–9

Daniel J. Estes

WILLIAM B. EERDMANS PUBLISHING COMPANY
GRAND RAPIDS, MICHIGAN / CAMBRIDGE, U.K.

Published 1997 in the U.K. by
APOLLOS (an imprint of Inter-Varsity Press)
and in the United States of America by
Wm. B. Eerdmans Publishing Co.
255 Jefferson Ave. S.E., Grand Rapids, Michigan 49503 /
P.O. Box 163, Cambridge CB3 9PU U.K.

Printed in the United States of America

01 00 99 98 97   7 6 5 4 3 2 1

Library of Congress Cataloging-in-Publication Data

Estes, Daniel J. 1953- .
Hear, my son : teaching and learning in Proverbs 1-9 / Daniel J. Estes.
p.   cm.   (New studies in biblical theology)
Includes bibliographical references and indexes.
ISBN 0-8028-4404-9 (pbk. : alk. paper)
1. Bible. O.T. Proverbs I-IX — Criticism, interpretation, etc.
2. Education in the Bible. I. Title. II. Series.
BS1465.6.E38E88   1997
223′.706 — dc21   97-31989
CIP

For Jonathan, my son,
truly a good gift from the Lord
(Psalm 127:3–5)

Contents

Series preface

New Studies in Biblical Theology is a series of monographs that address key issues in the discipline of biblical theology. Contributions to the series focus on one or more of three areas: 1. the nature and status of biblical theology, including its relations with other disciplines (*e.g.* historical theology, exegesis, systematic theology, historical criticism, narrative theology); 2. the articulation and exposition of the structure of thought of a particular biblical writer or corpus; and 3. the delineation of a biblical theme across all or part of the biblical corpora.

Above all, these monographs are creative attempts to help thinking Christians understand their Bibles better. The series aims simultaneously to instruct and to edify, to interact with the current literature, and to point the way ahead. In God's universe, mind and heart should not be divorced: in this series we will try not to separate what God has joined together. While the footnotes interact with the best of the scholarly literature, the text is uncluttered with untransliterated Greek and Hebrew, and tries to avoid too much technical jargon. The volumes are written within the framework of confessional evangelicalism, but there is always an attempt at thoughtful engagement with the sweep of the relevant literature.

This volume, the fourth in the series, is an exposition of prominent themes in Proverbs 1 – 9, dealing with what the French would call *formation*. Our English word 'education' doesn't quite catch it, as our word is a bit too restricted to the merely cerebral. Nevertheless, it is the holistic vision of 'instruction', of *formation*, that occupies the attention of Dr Estes. His work not only illumines some important chapters of the Old Testament, but serves as a salutary reminder for the people of God today to keep certain fundamental priorities clear.

D. A. Carson
Trinity Evangelical Divinity School,
Deerfield, Illinois

Preface

This monograph is the product of several years of reflection, research and discussion. It began as a paper for a seminary class, in which I used Proverbs 1 – 9 as a framework for constructing a biblically informed philosophy of education. In recent years I have studied Proverbs 1 – 9 in more detail in preparation for an honours seminar at Cedarville College, in which I compared and contrasted the implicit pedagogical theory in this biblical text with the explicit philosophy of education propounded in the writings of John Dewey. My students, with their keen questions and penetrating insights, have been a continual impetus to my own study.

When I was asked to contribute a volume to the *New Studies in Biblical Theology* series, this subject was my natural choice. I determined to research the considerable literature on Proverbs 1 – 9, as well as surveying related areas such as biblical wisdom and the wisdom of the ancient Near Eastern world. The parameters of the series have required that I summarize my argumentation at many points. Although that necessarily means a loss in thoroughness, the compensating gain in succinctness will doubtless make the study more useful to a wider audience.

I owe a great debt to many people who have supported me in this project. My series editor, Professor D. A. Carson, has been an inspiration by his ever-gracious support and his own stimulating example of scholarly excellence. I am grateful that the friendship which we began a decade ago in Cambridge, England, has been renewed through this endeavour. My colleagues at Cedarville College, especially within the Biblical Education department, have encouraged me through their cheerful words and faithful prayers. The library staffs at Cedarville College and at Trinity Lutheran Seminary have provided excellent facilities and assistance, which have enabled me to complete my research.

I am most grateful to my family, who have lived with this project for the last two years. My wife, Carol, has taught me much of what I know about teaching, and our children, Jonathan, Christiana and Joel, have been my first and most delightful students. They were continually in my mind throughout the research and writing of this book.

My prayer is that this study will glorify the Lord God, who is the source of all true wisdom and knowledge.

December 1996   *Daniel J. Estes*
                                              Cedarville College
                                                      Ohio

Abbreviations

BTB	*Biblical Theology Bulletin*
BZAW	Beihefte zur *Zeitschrift für die alttestamentliche Wissenschaft*
CBQ	*Catholic Biblical Quarterly*
CBQMS	*Catholic Biblical Quarterly*, Monograph Series
EQ	*Evangelical Quarterly*
HUCA	*Hebrew Union College Annual*
IDB	*The Interpreter's Dictionary of the Bible*
Int	*Interpretation*
JAOS	*Journal of the American Oriental Society*
JBL	*Journal of Biblical Literature*
JBR	*Journal of Bible and Religion*
JETS	*Journal of the Evangelical Theological Society*
JNSL	*Journal of Northwest Semitic Languages*
JSOT	*Journal for the Study of the Old Testament*
JSOTSupp	*Journal for the Study of the Old Testament*, Supplements
JTS	*Journal of Theological Studies*
LXX	The Septuagint (Greek version of the Old Testament)
MT	Masoretic text
NS	New series
OTS	*Oudtestamentlische Studiën*
SBLDS	Society of Biblical Literature Dissertation Series
TDOT	*Theological Dictionary of the Old Testament*
TynB	*Tyndale Bulletin*
VT	*Vetus Testamentum*
VTSupp	*Vetus Testamentum*, Supplements
ZAW	*Zeitschrift für die alttestamentliche Wissenschaft*

Introduction

Description of the study

Only rarely does the Bible speak systematically when it discusses theological, philosophical and ethical issues. For the most part the writers of the Scriptures addressed specific occasions that shaped the form in which the narratives, laws, oracles, poetry, epistles and wisdom utterances were communicated. When the present-day interpreter endeavours to move beyond the original context of the biblical data to consider more universal concerns, different modes of investigation must be used.

Even a cursory reading of the book of Proverbs reveals that it is dominated by the subject of education. The voice of the teacher addressing his pupils resounds from its pages. A wide array of topics is presented, and frequent exhortations challenge the learner to hear and heed the instruction from the teacher.

This material, however, comes for the most part without recognizable order or sequence. Much of Proverbs consists of apparently random collections of maxims. The reader sees many individual pieces, but the puzzle as a whole remains unclear.

This monograph endeavours to synthesize the unorganized data from a portion of the book of Proverbs into a more systematic statement of the pedagogical theory that underlies its teachings. In its biblical form, the pedagogy of this corpus is not explicit or structured, but implicit and unstructured. This study seeks to organize the data into seven categories typical of pedagogical discussion.

1. *Worldview*
   What assumptions shaped the concept of education in the wisdom tradition in which Proverbs 1 – 9 was written?

2. *Values*
   What attitudes and commitments were the pre-eminent concerns of Proverbs 1 – 9?
3. *Goals*
   According to Proverbs 1 – 9, what outcomes should education produce in the learner?
4. *Curriculum*
   What subject matter was taught to the learner?
5. *Instruction*
   What processes did the teacher use in instructing the learner?
6. *Teacher*
   What role or roles did the teacher play, and what was the nature of his responsibility in the educational endeavour?
7. *Learner*
   What role did the learner play in the accomplishment of a successful educational experience?

To the contemporary reader, the term 'education' often suggests a highly organized system, frequently controlled and financed by various levels of government, that equips the younger generation with the knowledge and skills necessary for useful service in the work-force. This study, however, uses the concept of education more in the sense of the French notion of *formation*, that is, for the development of the learner toward intellectual and ethical maturity. Proverbs 1 – 9 has much to say to this sense of education as personal formation.

This monograph is not primarily a work of exegesis, though it builds upon an extensive analysis of exegetical studies. It is not a historical reconstruction of the development of the extant texts, nor is it a literary analysis of its structural features. Though it is part of a theological series, its concern is not to fit the content of Proverbs into the traditional categories of systematic theology.

Instead, this study focuses on a single major unit of Proverbs, the first nine chapters. Working from the standard Hebrew text, it organizes the data into the seven pedagogical categories outlined above. As a result, it reconstructs a synthetic statement of the pedagogical theory that lies embedded in the text. By this procedure, the content of Proverbs 1 – 9 is used in a way that agrees with, but transcends, the original purpose of the text.

Modern literary convention uses gender-neutral language for reference to general human phenomena. This study follows that pattern when discussing education in non-specific contexts. It must be recognized, however, that Proverbs 1 – 9 most often uses distinctively masculine language, such as the frequent address 'my son', and it teaches by means of images, such as the women of wisdom and folly, that are particularly suited to communicate to an audience of young men. To use gender-neutral language when the text is speaking explicitly to young men introduces an anachronism that dulls the clarity of the textual meaning. Consequently, in this study neutral language will be used when possible, but when Proverbs 1 – 9 speaks to the learner as a young man, the masculine language of the text will be retained.

Rationale for the study

The first nine chapters of Proverbs gives ample evidence of being a discrete unit within the context of the extant book. This section is marked by extended discourses, which contrast with the individual proverbs that characterize the rest of the book. In addition, it is framed by the similar statements in Proverbs 1:7 and 9:10 which define the fundamental significance of the fear of Yahweh. Furthermore, the content of the section is more explicitly theological than the material found in the remainder of Proverbs. An additional striking feature is its frequent use of the address 'Hear, my son', which adds a strong didactic cast to its observations and exhortations. The introductory statement in Proverbs 1:1–7 may well have been composed to preface the entire book, but the notice in 10:1 certainly distinguishes Proverbs 1 – 9 from the collection that begins in chapter 10. For these reasons, it is appropriate to study this section as a unified composition.

Although scholars for the most part agree on the distinctness of Proverbs 1 – 9, they diverge widely on the question of its original date. Most contemporary scholars view these chapters as a redactional introduction that the final editors of the book composed in the post-exilic or even Hellenistic era (Cox 1993: 3). Two major lines of evidence are used to argue for the late dating of this section. Proverbs 1 – 9 uses longer literary units, whereas the rest of the book has a heavy concentration of couplets. Form criticism reasons that literary development proceeds from the simple to the complex. However, as Nel (1981b: 139–140) points out, this theory, though plausible, is not necessary.[1] Nel himself does hold to a post-exilic date for the section, but on theological rather than literary grounds. The theological line of evidence points to the content of Proverbs 1 – 9, in particular the personification or hypostasis of wisdom in Proverbs 1:20–33 and 8:22–31, as proof of its origination in the post-exilic community.

Although the majority of scholars have been persuaded by the literary and theological arguments for the post-exilic date of Proverbs 1 – 9, a pre-exilic date is championed by some. With regard to the literary aspects of the section, Kayatz (1966), Lang (1986) and Boström (1990) demonstrate that comparable literature from Egypt and Mesopotamia derives from the second millennium BC. Thus, the literary form of Proverbs 1 – 9 could well reflect the time of the united monarchy as the introductory notice in 1:1 purports. Kitchen analyses closely the literary affinities between Proverbs and its ancient Near Eastern parallels, and he concludes on the basis of the literary evidence that 'the most probable *literary* date of Solomon I [Proverbs 1 – 24] is entirely compatible with that of the named author in the title of the work, *i.e.*, king Solomon, of *c.* 950 BC' (1977: 99).

In a similar way, the theological argument for the post-exilic date of Proverbs 1 – 9 has also been questioned. As von Rad contends, the notion that intensive theological thought came to Israel only in the post-exilic period rests more on the theory of the evolutionary development of religion than it does on explicit evidence. He says:

> The proof that only in the post-exilic period could such teaching be given has still to be produced. Perhaps, with regard to the teachings of Prov. 1 – 9, we must simply think of different transmitters who, at the same time, stood in different teaching traditions (1972: 114).

[1] Nel argues: 'The method of handling stylistic forms of the proverb as a development from a single sentence into a two-membered sentence and eventually to a composition, sounds reasonable (form-critically), but it is not sufficient for the postulation of a linear development. The occurrence of greater semantic units does not indicate an evolutionary process. The smaller and the bigger units could have existed side by side.'

A further support for the early dating of the section is the implicit social setting that permeates it. The entire book of Proverbs reflects prosperity and optimism, which would certainly suit the affluent times of Solomon more than the impoverished post-exilic community. The wisdom sayings reflect a stable monarchy with a recognizable class system more closely than life under a Persian overlord (Fox 1968: 56–57).

The predominant scholarly position regarding the post-exilic date for Proverbs 1 – 9 rests on questionable assumptions about the development of literature and theology in ancient Israel. The parallel literary artefacts in Egypt and Mesopotamia predate Proverbs 1 – 9 by several centuries, which undermines the plausibility of extended literary compositions originating in Israel only after the exile. Similarly, concrete evidence for theological development of the concept of wisdom only in the post-exilic time has not been produced. The implicit social setting in the stable monarchy period suggests that, contrary to the common scholarly opinion, it might be most appropriate to read Proverbs within its purported setting in the time of Solomon, while recognizing that later editorial work, especially in the time of Hezekiah (Pr. 25:1), may have shaped the canonical form of the book.

Although the prehistory of the extant text of Proverbs may be debatable, what is certain is that from ancient times Proverbs 1- 9 has served as the opening section of the book. As a discrete unit it can be studied on its own terms, but at the same time it should also be viewed in terms of its connection to the rest of the book. In a thematic way, Proverbs 1 – 9 serves as a general overview of the subjects that Proverbs 10 – 31 explores in specific detail. This extended prologue to the book discusses in elegant portraits what the maxims of the body of Proverbs picture in quick snapshots. As Childs notes, Proverbs 1 – 9 is the prism through which the remainder of the book is read (1979: 552–553).

Both the discreteness of Proverbs 1 – 9 as a literary unit and its larger canonical dimension lend legitimacy to this study. Though it would be ideal to examine the complete corpus of wisdom literature in the Bible in order to discover its implicit pedagogical theory, that procedure would be both overwhelming and problematic. The biblical wisdom literature encompasses several complete books of the Bible, as well as portions of numerous other books. In addition, extensive extrabiblical sources would need to be analysed.[2] This investigation would also entail thorny, and probably insoluble, issues of literary history, for the wisdom corpus spans several centuries.

The present study is much more modest in scope, for it focuses only on Proverbs 1 – 9. It recognizes that this section in its canonical location functions as an overview of the themes and priorities of the book of Proverbs. Nevertheless, the specific purpose for this monograph is to identify what this particular portion of biblical literature says and implies about education.

Fox notes that though Proverbs 1 – 9 is clearly a didactic text, modern scholars have given only scant attention to the issues of pedagogy that it raises, preferring rather to view it in literary, philosophical or theological terms (1994: 233–234). This study endeavours to remedy that oversight. Its conclusions, however, are distinctive to Proverbs 1 – 9. Only thorough similar investigations of the other texts of the wisdom corpus could justify elevating the pedagogical philosophy of this section to the level of a paradigm of pedagogy for wisdom literature as a whole. Nevertheless, because Proverbs 1 – 9 functions canonically to introduce the book of Proverbs, it would not be surprising if a comprehensive analysis of the wisdom corpus were to support in large measure the implicit pedagogical theory found in Proverbs 1 – 9.

---

[2] A useful survey of wisdom literature with the history of its interpretation is found in J. Day *et al.* (eds.) (1995).

Chapter One

The worldview of Proverbs 1 – 9

No book is written in a vacuum, for every literary text is shaped by historical, cultural and sociological factors. Even more influential are the ideological assumptions, or the worldview, of the author. In order to understand the implicit pedagogical theory in Proverbs 1 – 9, one must first define the worldview which produced it. What were the assumptions that shaped the concept of education in the sense of personal formation in the wisdom tradition in which Proverbs was written?

Wilhelm Dilthey reasoned that humans have a world picture (*Weltbild*) that precedes a conscious view of the world. Upon reflection, this pre-theoretical picture is developed into a worldview (*Weltanschauung*) (Holmes 1983: 32). A worldview is not a full-blown philosophy of life, but the beliefs, attitudes and values that cause a person to see the world in a certain way. It is not a system of thought, but a perceptual framework for viewing the world (Walsh and Middleton 1984: 17). As Sire states, 'A world view is a set of presuppositions (assumptions which may be true, partially true or entirely false) which we hold (consciously or subconsciously, consistently or inconsistently) about the basic make-up of our world' (1988: 17).

It is evident that a worldview implies a prior faith commitment. Even in areas of life in which empirical testing is impossible, the worldview makes assertions about the nature of reality. From the question of the origin of life to the search for ultimate meaning, what one believes sets the course for how all of the world is viewed. Of course, this worldview must in time be evaluated and validated so that it can provide a solid epistemological foundation for life. Nevertheless, it is important to recognize that even apart from verification a worldview is a powerful force in shaping the actions, attitudes and values of an individual or a society. To understand how education was conceived in ancient Israel, then, one must first determine how

Israel's concept of teaching and learning was shaped by its view of the world.

Sire (1988:18) helpfully describes a worldview in terms of the answers to the following questions:

1. What is prime reality – the really real?
2. What is the nature of external reality, that is, the world around us?
3. What is a human being?
4. What happens to a person at death?
5. Why is it possible to know anything at all?
6. How do we know what is right and wrong?
7. What is the meaning of human history?

Not all of these questions impinge directly on Proverbs 1 – 9. The discussion in this chapter will summarize the worldview of this section of Proverbs in four general propositions that appear to be of special significance in the shaping of pedagogy in the wisdom tradition.

It is crucial to realize that a worldview is not just a description of how one sees life as it actually is. It also provides a vision for seeing life as it ideally ought to be. 'Our world view determines our values. It helps us interpret the world around us. It sorts out what is important from what is not, what is of highest value from what is least' (Walsh and Middleton 1984: 32). In other words, the worldview of Proverbs 1 – 9 was a powerful causative factor in resolving issues such as the values and goals of education, the curriculum, and how the teacher and the learner relate to one another. There is an integral relationship between the assumptions that shaped the worldview of ancient Israel and the concept of education that developed in that society.

From the time of Solomon onward ancient Israel was profoundly involved in international affairs. Politically, Israel entered into alliance with foreign powers, sometimes with Egypt to the south, and at other times with the Mesopotamian powers of Assyria and Babylon. Commerce forged numerous links with other cultures in the Mediterranean world and beyond.

It is not surprising, therefore, that the biblical wisdom literature includes language and concepts that parallel what is found in Egyptian and Mesopotamian texts. Where Israel's worldview was compatible with that of its neighbours, the concepts were integrated into the biblical wisdom corpus with little material change. What typically happened, however, was that Israel borrowed language and concepts generated within other worldviews, and then adapted them to fit into its own view of the world (von Rad 1972: 5). Just as a speaker may well use a quotation from an author without suggesting total agreement with the originator, so Proverbs uses material that may have originated with Egyptian and Mesopotamian scribes, but in a way that fits into the biblical worldview.

Although Proverbs does share many resemblances with its ancient Near Eastern neighbours, it is most fundamentally connected to the rest of the Hebrew Bible. As Waltke concludes,

> . . . the sages and the prophets were true spiritual yokefellows sharing the same Lord, cultus, faith, hope, anthropology and epistemology, speaking with the same authority, and making similar religious and ethical demands on their hearers. In short, they drank from the same spiritual well (1979b: 304).

This unity of thought with the rest of the Hebrew Scriptures, however, is not demonstrated by explicit reference to prescriptions of the law or the acts of salvation history. Proverbs has a different agenda from that of the Torah and the prophets. Its ethical message builds upon the assumed base of theology that was already known to the hearers (Craigie 1979: 8). Just as a text in calculus presupposes familiarity with algebra without necessarily making overt reference to it, so the pedagogy of Proverbs assumes that the reader shares its worldview and only rarely makes explicit reference to what is taught elsewhere in the Bible. Whybray concludes rightly:

> There is nothing here which is contradictory to the public affirmations of salvation-faith found elsewhere in the Old Testament, and there is no reason to suppose that that historic faith was not taken for granted by its authors (1994b: 10).

Creation: The universe is Yahweh's creation

The most fundamental assumption of the worldview represented in Proverbs 1 – 9 is that the universe is Yahweh's creation.
The world did not come into being because of a primeval
struggle between rival deities. Neither was it the product of
impersonal time and chance. Instead, the whole world which
exists at the present time was created by Yahweh alone.

It has often been claimed that Israel's wisdom traditions
developed from early secular sayings that were reinterpreted
and recast with theological language. Crenshaw (1981a: 92)
agrees in part that Israel's later wisdom literature is more
theological in its content, but he points out rightly that 'this
editing process must surely have found a kindred base upon
which to work. It follows that wisdom contained a religious
element from the beginning'. In fact, the parts of Israel's
wisdom tradition that include the greatest concentration of
theological language can be compared with Egyptian parallels
that predate the purported secular portions of Old Testament
wisdom. It is more appropriate, therefore, to view the biblical
wisdom literature 'as the unfolding of a philosophy and worldview which did not change in essentials' (Eaton 1989: 4).

It appears, then, that Old Testament wisdom was always
theologically grounded, even though its theological language
may have become more or less explicit in different times and
genres. In addition, though the wisdom literature had its own
emphases that distinguished it from the legal, prophetic and
hymnic literature, its worldview reflected the understanding of
reality shared by all Israelites (Murphy 1981c: 3). Wisdom is
therefore a form of instruction that is not incompatible with the
law and the prophets, but is complementary to the rest of the
biblical texts (Wilson 1987: 330).

This worldview sees all of reality as a universe. Yahweh's
creation encompasses the entire world, for he is the maker of
heaven and earth, not merely a limited tribal deity. Though he
did indeed initiate a special covenant relationship with Israel,
Yahweh is Lord over all of the nations, for he has created all of
the earth.

Because the entire universe has its source in the creative
activity of Yahweh, there is a common ethical system that applies
to all humans. Clements observes:

Beyond the ethic of the clan and of the nation, wisdom established an ethic grounded in creation itself and valid for all humanity. It addressed its teachings to persons as members of the human race, and not as members of a specific clan, or even a national community (1990: 25).

In agreement with both narrative and poetic biblical accounts, Proverbs asserts that Yahweh created the world. Proverbs 3:19–20 places Yahweh at centre stage by positioning his name, rather than the customary verb, as the first word in the statement (Whybray 1994: 68). The verbs 'founded' and 'established' are standard terms used to describe divine creative activity.[1] As the creator, Yahweh is actively involved in the world which he made. In contrast to deistic notions of an absent designer, Yahweh brought about the flood as judgment upon the earth in the time of Noah (*cf.* Gn. 7:11). In a beneficent vein, he prompts the skies to water the earth so that the crops may grow.

Proverbs 8:22–31 views the time that preceded the divine creation. The major focus of this passage is the function of wisdom in the created order, but it also speaks of the creator as the one who fashioned the entire universe and who pre-dates it all (Boström 1990: 148). Far from being a hypostasis,[2] wisdom is regarded as being established, or installed (*cf.* Ps. 2:6), by Yahweh (Alden 1983: 73–74). Wisdom is not his rival, but a tool in his hands.

Nevertheless, the crucial role of wisdom in Yahweh's creation must not be neglected. Proverbs 3:19 states that Yahweh founded the earth by wisdom and set the heavens in place by understanding. Within the same passage the teacher exclaims, 'Blessed is the man who finds wisdom, the man who gains understanding' (3:13). This collocation indicates that '. . . the wisdom that directs life is the same wisdom that created the universe; to surrender to God's wisdom is to put oneself in harmony with creation, the world around one' (Ross 1991: 919).

---

[1] Perdue (1994: 79) discusses four metaphors used in Proverbs 1 – 9 to describe Yahweh's creation and maintenance of the world: architect (3:19–20), city (1:20–21; 8:1–3), house (9:1–6) and birth (8:22–31).

[2] This subject is discussed in length in the major commentaries on Proverbs. Kidner (1964: 78–79) offers a succinct rationale for regarding this reference as a personification rather than as a hypostasis.

As has been noted already, the main feature of Proverbs 8:22–31 is the presence of wisdom during Yahweh's creative activity. Two thorny interpretive issues are determinative for understanding the significance of wisdom in creation. First, the verb *qānâ* in verse 22 has been translated 'created' (Ross 1991: 946; Cohen 1952: 48) or 'possessed' (Scott 1965: 71–72; Whybray 1994b: 130, with reservations). The uses of *qānâ* in Proverbs 1:5, 4:5 and 7 support the sense of 'possess', such that wisdom was an attribute of Yahweh that guided his creation of the world.

The second term, *'āmôn*, in 8:30, has prompted renderings of 'craftsman' (Kidner 1964: 80–81; Delitzsch 1971: 191), 'nursling' (Aitken 1986: 83; Whybray 1994b: 135) and, less likely, 'binding together' (Scott 1965: 72).[3] Throughout this passage wisdom is pictured as being with Yahweh as his companion during his creation, but not as an active agent of the creative work. The repeated verb 'give birth' in 8:24–25 fits better the image of a child than it does a craftsman. It seems more appropriate therefore to adopt the sense of nursling, or young child, for *'āmôn*.[4]

When the high poetry of Proverbs 8:22–31 is reduced to prose, wisdom emerges as the divinely ordained order that permeates God's world.[5] Yahweh embedded wisdom in his creation, so only through wisdom can one discern how to live successfully in his world (Boström 1990: 53–54). As Garrett notes, '. . . if the very universe is made in accordance with the

---

[3] Excellent discussions of the interpretive options can be found in Farmer (1991: 54–55) and Scott (1965: 72).

[4] Fox (1996: 699–702) argues well that the term is an infinitive absolute meaning 'being raised/growing up', which serves as an adverbial complement to the main verb of Proverbs 8:30. Thus, he concludes (702): 'Lady Wisdom is declaring that while God was busy creating the world, she was nearby, growing up like a child in his care (v. 30a) and giving him delight (v. 30bα) by playing before him (v. 30bβ) in the world that would be inhabited (v. 31a). Now that humans are on the scene, *she* is the guardian and teacher and declares, "And my delight is in mankind" (v. 31b).'

[5] Clements (1990: 19) observes well: 'Hitherto the almost exclusive concern of scholars with this cosmic role of wisdom has been with its personification as a female figure, possibly originally as a goddess, and with the femininity of wisdom. Yet this was certainly not the central intellectual feature that has motivated the development of this imagery, and may have been little more than a convenient literary device. In fact, the primary feature of this poem celebrating the role of wisdom in creation is the strong emphasis that it places upon the cosmic range and authority of wisdom.'

principles of Wisdom, it is folly for anyone to live contrary to those principles' (1993: 109).

Implicit in the assumption that the universe is Yahweh's creation is the conviction that human meaning is found only in relationship to the creator. Because Yahweh created the world in a purposeful way, the world is not random and meaningless. The order that God established when he made the world provides the ground for human significance in the cosmos. Holmes reasons that a person's meaning is found in the relationship between the human and the Maker, for 'God is the source not only of all being but also of value, hope, and purpose' (1983: 62). In the wisdom literature, this relationship is delineated under the rubric of the fear of Yahweh, which is the beginning of wisdom (Pr. 9:10).

A final implication of the premise of the divine creation of the world is that there is no legitimate division between sacred and secular spheres of life. The world as created by Yahweh is a universe in which the divine order permeates each part. The teacher does not hesitate to draw insights from observations of nature, for the activity of the ant (Pr. 6:6–8) is maintained by God's order just as is the activity of humans. Since Yahweh's creation 'underlies all reality, also what moderns call the secular is part of God's domain' (Malchow 1983: 112).

The modern dichotomy between secular life and religious faith, or between the profane and the sacred, is foreign to the worldview of biblical wisdom. In Proverbs, the juxtaposition of the routine details of daily life with reminders of Yahweh's evaluation of those activities (*cf.* Pr. 3:27–35) reveals that all of life is regarded as a seamless fabric. As O'Conner comments:

> . . . ordinary life and the life of faith are not two separate spheres but one unified experience of God's creation. When Israel's wisdom literature concentrates intensely on mundane human concerns, it is not ignoring faith but assuming it (1988: 16–17).

Order: Yahweh is sovereignly controlling the world

The worldview of Proverbs begins with the assumption that Yahweh was the sole creator of the universe. In addition, it holds that Yahweh's control over the world is continuing, active and personal. Because of this, the world is not driven about by erratic, arbitrary and accidental forces, but it is maintained and directed by the order which Yahweh established at creation. Right from the beginning Yahweh willed that the world be stable and orderly (Brueggemann 1972: 23).

This divine order for the world functions at several levels. The physical world manifests purposeful design from the intricate movements of the celestial objects to the complex interrelationships among diverse ecosystems. Moreover, as Proverbs teaches repeatedly, there is a predictable relationship between acts and consequences which holds true in most situations in life. This order encouraged the search by wise teachers to regulate life in accordance with the intrinsic order of the universe. Yahweh has already constructed the world with pervasive orderliness, so 'each human being must accept the fact that the world is put together this way and must learn to live accordingly' (Barré 1981: 41).

In the thought of Proverbs, wisdom is skill in living according to Yahweh's order.[6] Folly is choosing to live contrary to the order which he embedded in the universe. Just as wisdom was present at the creation as Yahweh established his structure for the world (Pr. 8:22–31), so each person is obliged to live by wisdom if success is to be achieved. As Matlack notes:

> Wisdom is in this sense a kind of orderly mean-
> ingfulness structuring creation. If you attempt to live
> by its guidelines and submit to its strictures, then you

[6] As Nel (1982: 112) reasons, Yahweh's moral order rules out human autonomy: 'Subordination to the created order means in fact re-established order in human conduct. Accordingly man cannot autonomously design his own ethical imperative, but the ethical imperative heteronomously originates in God, the creator of order. Thus, wisdom's morality is not autonomous, but on the contrary, it is diametrically opposed to Greek and philosophical ethics which ascribe priority to man's reason. Human conscience cannot be the starting point for knowledge of good and evil.'

will do well. This principle would not work unless it was implanted by God in the very act of creation (1988: 427).

A basic contention of the wisdom literature is that the divine order in the world is knowable, at least in part. The proverbs frequently draw lessons from nature as well as from observations of social behaviour. For example, in Proverbs 6:6 the wise teacher exhorts his student, 'Go to the ant, you sluggard; consider its ways and be wise!' Lessons drawn from the animal world were part of the repertoire of Solomon (1 Ki. 4:33), and they can be found in numerous passages of the Old Testament (*cf.* Jb. 12:7; Is. 1:3; Je. 8:7; Whybray 1994b: 96).

If order can be learned through observation of the world, then it can also be taught. Consequently, the curriculum of wisdom focuses on life, for in observing life the student can become adept at recognizing how Yahweh constructed his world. In discerning this wisdom, the individual is equipped to function successfully in life.

It is crucial to remember that the divine order for the world derives from the righteous character of Yahweh. There is moral governance in the universe because God's justice directs and delimits all that he does. Wisdom, then, is not amoral pragmatism, which alleges that whatever works is right. Living wisely in Yahweh's world is living according to his justice.

This fact is demonstrated in Proverbs 5:21–22. In warning the learner against the allurements of the adulteress, the teacher gives this rationale: 'For a man's ways are in full view of the LORD, and he examines all his paths' (5:21). Lest this be construed as speaking merely of divine omniscience and not divine governance, the teacher speaks of the righteous standard by which human deeds will be recompensed: 'The evil deeds of a wicked man ensnare him; the cords of his sin hold him fast' (5:22). Waltke notes well that 'wisdom must be thought of as a broad, theological concept denoting a fixed, righteous order to which the wise man submits his life' (1979a: 238).

The sovereign control of the world by Yahweh means that the wise life conforms to the norm of his righteousness. He has given to humans the ability to perceive the order which he maintains. As they live in accordance with this order, they 'follow wisdom's path to justice, knowledge, and well-being' (Perdue

1993: 75). It is Yahweh's righteousness which provides the standard by which human government maintains justice in society (Eaton 1989: 4).

Just as Yahweh created the world, so he himself sustains order in it. The act of creation was not merely the initiation of an ongoing process of existence. Personified wisdom states that it was present when Yahweh 'gave the sea its boundary so that the waters would not overstep his command . . .' (Pr. 8:29), but Yahweh's involvement with the world did not cease with his original creative activity. The wisdom literature, including both the practical wisdom of Proverbs and the speculative wisdom works of Job and Ecclesiastes, affirms that Yahweh continues to be alive and active in the world (McKenzie 1967: 4; Duhaime 1980: 195).

Proverbs 8:31 substantiates this point, for it presents wisdom as 'rejoicing in his whole world'. It is Yahweh's world, the universe which he created and which he sustains, in which wisdom finds its delight. Biblical wisdom, then, at its heart holds to the ongoing control of Yahweh over the world.

Because Yahweh himself sustains order in his world, the world is governed by a personal agent, not propelled by impersonal forces. Many scholars have drawn parallels between the concept of *Maat* in the Egyptian wisdom literature and the sense of the order of the world evident in biblical wisdom. In Egyptian thought *Maat* was the order which Re instituted when he overcame chaos. The pharaohs were god-kings who governed society by this static order. The responsibility of each person was to conform to this order across the full range of activities (Fox 1968: 58). The society in Egypt was regarded as perfect in its inception, so history becomes simply 'the inevitable working-out of its original and immutable constitution' (McKane 1970: 58). The continuing involvement of the deity, therefore, was unnecessary, for humans merely worked out the details of the unalterable plan.

It is undeniable that there are significant similarities between *Maat* and the concept of order in the biblical wisdom. Both recognize the divine source of order in the world. Both acknowledge the need for humans to live in accordance with this order if they are to prove successful. Both insist that the order encompasses all areas of existence, making it the foundation for personal and societal life. In fact, Emerton's description of *Maat* could easily serve for the biblical sense of order as well: '. . . this order is manifest in nature in the normalcy of phenomena; it is manifest in society as justice; and it is manifest in an individual's life as truth' (1979b: 215).

Boström, however, raises some legitimate objections to an essential linkage between *Maat* and biblical order. He argues that Egyptologists themselves are beginning to entertain different notions of *Maat*, viewing it as a concept which changed over time in Egypt (1990: 95). Furthermore, the Egyptian concept of *Maat* viewed order as an impersonal governing principle, in distinction from the biblical worldview which posits Yahweh as the active, personal director of history (1990: 93).

Even the sections of Proverbs which have been deemed by scholars as the most 'secular' contain clear witness to Yahweh's personal involvement in the world. For example, Proverbs 16:1 states, 'To man belong the plans of the heart, but from the LORD comes the reply of the tongue.' In a similar vein, Proverbs 21:31 observes, 'The horse is made ready for the day of battle, but victory rests with the LORD.' According to the biblical worldview, there is much predictability in the world which Yahweh has ordered, but he maintains his personal involvement so that the consequences of human actions may not always be anticipated. It seems best, therefore, to conclude with Murphy: 'Although some characteristics of *maat*. . . appear in the biblical description of wisdom, there is no justification for transferring the Egyptian experience of reality to Israel' (1970: 228).

It is important, then, to define carefully what order implies in the worldview of Proverbs 1 – 9. When Yahweh created the universe he embedded within it elements of causality and predictability. Through observation humans can discern the ways in which Yahweh has structured the world, and teach these patterns to others. The universe is not arbitrary, for Yahweh has constructed it with recognizable design. Neither is the world amoral, for Yahweh's order is intimately related to his righteous character.[7]

In addition to creating the world, Yahweh also sustains order in the world which he made. Unlike the Egyptian concept of

---

[7] As Waltke (1979b: 314) notes, Proverbs agrees with the rest of the Old Testament in affirming that 'Yahweh as the Judge of all men will reward the righteous and punish transgressors.'

Maat, which reflected a worldview assuming a closed, static world, biblical wisdom viewed Yahweh as personally involved in the ongoing progress of history. As Holmes concludes, 'The world should not therefore be thought of just mechanistically, in terms of impersonal causal mechanisms, even of mechanisms created by God, for a living and loving God remains active in it' (1983: 64). The world is ordered, because Yahweh is sovereignly controlling the world which he created.

Rationality: Yahweh's world is knowable, but also mysterious

Because Yahweh created the world and he is sovereignly controlling it, the world is knowable, at least in part. The universe manifests intelligent design in its order. This fact is the foundation for human understanding in the cosmos.

Yahweh planted truth within his universe, and he endowed humans with the capacity to discover it by using their intelligence (Crenshaw 1981a: 209). In fact, wisdom is portrayed as calling out to humans, seeking to elicit their attention and response. This invitation is addressed to all humans, regardless of social class (Pr. 8:4).[8] Wisdom utters its cry at the gates, the centre of public life in the ancient city (Pr. 1:20–21; 8:1–3). As Cox notes,

> Wisdom is competing for attention in precisely that arena where people live their lives, and where they are already preoccupied with affairs. Wisdom's place is thus not the ivory tower, but the arena of daily life, and she wishes to become involved with mankind at every level (1982b: 148).

This call is clearly heard by all, for the rhetorical question which introduces the invitation in Proverbs 8:1 has the force of a strong positive assertion (Farmer 1991: 51; Whybray 1994b: 122).

This appeal, however, must be answered by a conscious, decisive commitment to acquire wisdom. As Proverbs 4:7

---

[8] Cohen (1952: 44), comparing Ps. 49:3, defines *'îšîm* as those possessing high social status and *bᵉnê 'ādām* as a term for the masses.

teaches, the beginning of wisdom is a decision to get it, even at the cost of all that one possesses. The search for wisdom, then, is not a supplement, but it must be a radical reorientation of life, in which wisdom becomes the prime priority. Wisdom promises much to those who seek it, but it also requires 'constancy of allegiance and affection' (McKane 1970: 305).

This commitment is pictured as an intensive search for precious metals. In four lines ascending to a climax, this search is seen to require perseverance, diligence and hard work (Pr. 2:3–4).[9] Just as miners go to heroic efforts in locating and extracting ore from the earth (cf. Jb. 28:1–11), so wisdom is found only by those willing to put forth the same painstaking effort. Aitken remarks well: 'Neither silver ore nor wisdom is got in a day, or got without industry; but for miner and student alike, the prize is worth the toil. But toil there is; and so an earnest desire to obtain wisdom must be uppermost' (1986: 27).

In practical terms, the search for wisdom involves careful observation of life through personal experience and through the experiences of others as passed down through teachers. In life actions are repeated, and similar consequences recur. The wise person generalizes from observation of recurrent patterns, in order to formulate rational explanations for life in Yahweh's world.[10] These patterns serve then as guideposts for making wise choices (Scott 1965: xvii).

The wisdom tradition gathered these observations into a traditional corpus of tested information. Instead of each person

---

[9] Ross (1991: 912) notes well: 'The elevation in the lines from "call out" to "cry aloud" suggests that, if understanding does not come immediately, one should put forth greater efforts. So the ear hears the teaching, the mind understands what is said, and the voice is used to inquire for true knowledge. This search for wisdom and understanding should be as diligent as the search for precious metal (v. 4, "silver"), the simile suggesting both the value of the treasure and the diligence of the search.'

[10] Bloomfield (1984: 19) develops the significance of this emphasis of wisdom in the larger context of intellectual history: 'We must understand that wisdom is man's first and most basic step towards rationality. Out of it came the fundamental world-view of science before statistical principles redefined the notion of science in our century and for many people it is still the basic view. It was the drive to overcome the arbitrariness of things that led to the discovery or, in some cases, invention, of order underlying the apparent disorder and chance of the universe. Repetition occurs in nature and life and thus some kind of order can encompass the apparent irrationality of things.'

having to discover wisdom through individual experience, the teachers of wisdom accumulated the insights which the past generations had observed. Thus, each new generation inherited the aggregate wisdom of its ancestors, but it also was challenged to continue the process of observation so that succeeding generations would be the beneficiaries of its searching for wisdom.

Wisdom is learned through the observation of life and through the reception of tradition. The exhortation to observe the ant leads to a moral for human behaviour (Pr. 6:6–11). Just as the ant demonstrates foresight and diligence in securing its food supply without supervision to compel it, so the sluggard needs to discipline himself so as to prevent future ruin. A similar approach is used in the realm of human behaviour, when the teacher rehearses the allurement and destruction of a young man by the strange woman (Pr. 7) as a pre-emptive warning to his pupil.

Traditional wisdom is transmitted both by parents and by teachers. The paired references to father and mother in Proverbs 1:8 and 6:20 are unique to Hebrew wisdom literature in comparison with the ancient literature of Egypt and Mesopotamia (Whybray 1994b: 37). It is likely that most of the frequent references in Proverbs 1 – 9 to father and son fit best into the teacher-pupil relationship. Nevertheless, the explicit reference to the mother in these verses makes it plausible that the home was a significant contributor to the education of the young in ancient Israel.

The instruction in Proverbs 4:1–9 gives a glimpse into the transmission of truth. The teacher calls upon his pupils to hear the instruction which he, as their intellectual and moral father, is giving to them. This teaching is not original with him, for it is *leqaḥ*, traditional information transmitted from past generations (Cohen 1952: 21). He proceeds to cite the words of his father or teacher in 4:4–9, and thereby gives increased credibility to his appeal.

As the wisdom teachers observe the world, their attention turns from seeing *what* is in the world to explaining *why* actions typically produced predictable results. The question of causality assumes that the world possesses inherent order, which is a prerequisite for rational thinking (Bloomfield 1984: 20; Toombs 1988: 8–9). The wisdom teachers attempt to understand how the order in Yahweh's world functions, so that they can define the relation between acts and consequences.

This rational order in the world is presented in numerous forms. For example, Proverbs 3:1–12 contains six pairs of causes with corresponding consequences. If the learner fulfils the protasis, then the apodosis is certain to follow. Proverbs 5:8–14 gives a warning (8) followed by consequences which justify the warning (9–14). These consequences include personal exploitation, regret and public disgrace (Kidner 1964: 70). The teacher substantiates his prohibition in Proverbs 7:25 with the dire consequences which follow (7:26–27). On a positive note, the person who finds wisdom (3:13) is blessed by its beneficent rewards (3:14–18).

Many of the statements in Proverbs 1 – 9 present actions as pregnant with inherent consequences for good or evil. McKane argues from this that 'the relationship between the actions of the fools and the bad end which overtakes them is inward and necessary, not superimposed as the consequence of a forensic verdict and penalty' (1970: 271), which he relates to the impersonal concept of *Maat* in Egyptian wisdom literature.

It is true that a passage such as Proverbs 1:10–19 does not include explicit reference to divine retribution. On the other hand, Proverbs 2:21–22 points to a moral dimension embedded in consequences, for the upright will live in the land, but the wicked will be cut off from it. In Proverbs 5:21–23 an explicit statement of divine causality (21) juxtaposed with human responsibility (22–23) suggests that consequences are ultimately determined by Yahweh's governance of the world, even when they are not specifically stated as such in the text. Though reference to the divine dimension is not always at the fore, it is justifiable to conclude that 'wisdom then is the fixed cause-effect order that God created and upholds . . .' (Waltke 1987: 73). Even in a passage such as Proverbs 1:10–19, in which Yahweh is not at all mentioned, his moral order directs life in such a way that evil actions reap evil consequences (Hubbard 1989: 54).[11]

---

[11] Boström (1990: 116) argues reasonably that even formally impersonal statements of act and consequence do not necessarily rule out divine governance: '. . . the causation of the destruction of the wrong-doer was viewed in a variety of ways. The relationship between life-style and fate was indeed regarded as close, but the predisposition for the passive formulation of especially the negative judgments neither necessitates nor justifies the

At the same time that the wisdom literature demonstrates the causal relationship between acts and consequences, it also teaches that some of life is inscrutable. Although Proverbs 1 – 9 does not yield clear examples of this teaching, the larger corpus of wisdom includes sayings such as these: 'A man's steps are directed by the LORD. How then can anyone understand his own way?' (Pr. 20:24), and 'There is no wisdom, no insight, no plan that can succeed against the LORD' (Pr. 21:30). Taken together with the predominant witness to divine retribution, Proverbs portrays Yahweh as governing the world in justice, but also remaining free to act in ways which are inscrutable to humans (Whybray 1994b: 11). In describing how Yahweh typically acts, wisdom does not domesticate him into total predictability.[12]

Because Yahweh is just, both in his essential character and in his actions, his rule is not arbitrary, even though it is not always knowable. What transpires in his world may not appear to be logical to humans. It must be remembered, however, that 'logic itself is subject to God's law' so 'to elevate logic to the level of the norm for all creation is implicitly to assert its autonomy, to deny that *all things* (including logical thought) are subject to God's law' (Walsh and Middleton 1984: 177). Yahweh does not have to submit to the canons of human logic as he governs the universe which he created.

The sense of mystery which humans necessarily have as they seek to understand the world impels them to faith in Yahweh,

---

introduction of an impersonal concept of order or of a strict causal nexus between actions and consequences. Our view is that the passive formulation was favoured because it left every possibility open for the impending destruction of the wicked.'

[12] Yahweh's ordered world remains mysterious in part to humans because human knowledge is limited. Humans, though possessing rationality because they are made in the image of God (Gn. 1:26–27), are finite, ever deficient of the omniscience of God. In addition, the noetic effects of fallenness distort that which humans do see, so that they are unable to construe it accurately (1 Cor. 2:14; 2 Cor. 4:3–4). The problem of finiteness in all humans, and the additional problem of fallenness in unregenerate humans, are necessary limitations on their ability to understand the world. This human disability, however, should not call into question the viability of Yahweh's ordered universe. Rather, it is better to affirm that 'there is indeed a cosmic order but the human mind cannot grasp all of its ramifications, even those which impinge upon human experience' (Bergant 1984: 17, in agreement with von Rad).

which gives stability for life. Wisdom does not deny mystery or avoid it, but rather wisdom embraces Yahweh, who alone knows the world exhaustively. The fact that life cannot be explained and secured by human effort alone prompts humans to place their trust in the Lord, for it is the fear of Yahweh which is the beginning of wisdom (Pr. 9:10).

Fear of Yahweh: Humans must reverence Yahweh in their lives

The expression 'the fear of Yahweh'[13] frames Proverbs 1 – 9, occurring both near the beginning of the section (1:7) and near the end (9:10) to form an inclusio. In addition, the expression also occurs in 1:29; 2:5; 3:7; and 8:13. Thus, the significance of the term is indicated both by its frequency and by its positioning in the section.

This emphasis on the fear of Yahweh is not unique to Proverbs 1 – 9, however, for it is a key concept throughout the wisdom literature. In Proverbs 10 – 31 the expression and close parallels are used twelve times. Especially significant is the final reference in Proverbs 31:30, which states: 'Charm is deceptive, and beauty is fleeting; but a woman who fears the LORD is to be praised.' In the larger structure of Proverbs the virtuous woman fulfils the challenge set forth in the thesis of the book in 1:7.

The other biblical wisdom books also contain significant uses of 'the fear of Yahweh', or the comparable expressions 'fear of God [Elohim]' or 'fear of the Lord [Adonai]'. Job is described both by the narrator and by Yahweh as one who fears God (Jb. 1:1, 8; 2:3). The majestic hymn to wisdom concludes with the word of God to humans, 'The fear of the LORD [Adonai] – that is wisdom, and to shun evil is understanding' (Jb. 28:28). Furthermore, Ecclesiastes ends with this word of instruction: 'Now all has been heard; here is the conclusion of the matter; Fear God [Elohim] and keep his commandments, for this is the whole duty of man' (Ec. 12:13). Though the literary history of each of these books has been debated extensively, what is evident is that in their canonical form from antiquity all three

---

[13] Among the many useful studies of the fear of Yahweh are Fuhs (*TDOT* VI:290–315); Blocher (1977); Brongers (1948); Cox (1982a); and Derousseaux (1970).

major wisdom books maintain that the fear of Yahweh (Elohim/Adonai) is the key principle for wisdom (Blocher 1977: 5).[14]

The fear of Yahweh is an implication of his creation of the universe. Because Yahweh alone fashioned the world, all of life proceeds from him. Yahweh, then, is the foundational authority for the whole ethical system of wisdom. As Craigie remarks, 'Hebrew moral wisdom presupposes the existence of God, which in turn gives the whole system coherence, authority and integrity' (1979: 8).

If everything in the universe is dependent upon Yahweh, the sovereign creator, then nothing should be interpreted independently from him. According to Hebrew wisdom, the notion of the autonomy of human reason is false, for Yahweh's creation of the world means that 'it is consequently impossible to obtain an understanding of man's place in the design and purpose of living without a humble approach to Him' (Cohen 1952: 3).

As Proverbs 1:7b states, only a fool would ignore the creator and endeavour to live in opposition to his moral will. The creative order mandates that the proper stance for humans is humble submission to the ethical demands of the just God, rather than arrogant insistence on choosing their own way independent of the Lord who made them.

In the wisdom tradition, knowledge is not divorced from faith, but its ultimate connection with Yahweh the creator is always affirmed. The existence and authority of Yahweh are constantly in view, so that no division between the sacred and the secular spheres of life is allowed. Instead, 'every act bore religious consequences and arose from a religious understanding of reality. Life with people was at the same time existence in God's presence' (Crenshaw 1981a: 24).

Because every facet of life has a religious dimension, wisdom calls its hearers to a whole-life response to Yahweh. In this worldview every action and choice in life, including even the most apparently mundane, is imbued with theological significance. In other words, service to God is not a part of a person's

---

[14] Aitken (1986: 14–15) notes that the theme of the fear of Yahweh is important throughout the Old Testament, both in the sense of awe (Ex. 3:6), and of obedience to the divine law (Dt. 6:2).

agenda, but it flavours the entire agenda of life.[15]

The term 'fear' (*yir'â*) in the Old Testament can refer to dread (Dt. 2:25) or terror (Jon. 1:10, 16), or more positively to awe or reverence. The expression 'the fear of Yahweh' combines the senses of 'shrinking back in fear and of drawing close in awe' (Ross 1991: 907). This response is not abject terror which causes humans to cringe before Yahweh, but a sense of awe before the exalted Lord, such as Isaiah experienced when he saw the vision of Yahweh in the temple (Is. 6:1–5).

Awe before Yahweh precludes arrogant defiance of the creator or flippant disregard of his moral demands (Barré 1981: 42). Instead, the fear of Yahweh is profound respect which causes the human to acknowledge creaturely dependence upon him. The one who fears Yahweh admits that the Lord alone possesses total knowledge and control in the universe he has made. Rather than questioning or rejecting the dictates of Yahweh, the reverential worshipper adopts the position of the submissive servant before him.

Even when it is not stated explicitly, the fear of Yahweh governs the thoughts of Proverbs 1 – 9 (Brueggemann 1972: 40). It is the critical initial point which necessarily affects all of life. As Clements notes rightly, 'this was the indispensable first step of commitment without which the voice of wisdom could not be heard' (1992: 156).

Proverbs 3:7 draws an antithesis between fearing Yahweh, which causes one to turn away from evil, and being wise in one's own eyes. Wisdom chooses to renounce autonomy and to place its trust in Yahweh. Instead of pursuing personal preferences, the wise person places confidence in Yahweh's direction.

The fear of Yahweh as the crucial principle for wisdom indicates that in biblical wisdom knowledge is impossible

---

[15] Speaking more generally of a biblical worldview, Walsh and Middleton (1984: 67–68) declare: 'The paths of wisdom-obedience and folly-disobedience cut across everything we do. We are called to serve the Lord and acknowledge his kingship in the whole range of our cultural activities. There are no sacred-secular compartments here. Our service to God is not something we do *alongside* our ordinary human life. The Bible knows no such dichotomy. In the biblical world view all of life, in all of its dimensions, is constituted as religion. From our economic choices to our recreation, from our prayer life to the way in which we bathe our babies, in every cultural action and deed, we live only in response to the cosmic, creation law of God. This is God's universe throughout. And we are called to be responsible respondents to his overarching Torah.'

without belief. In other words, it teaches that faith seeks understanding. At the same time, Proverbs 2:5 states that the fear of Yahweh is also the consequence of the search for wisdom. The paradox which this suggests is more apparent than real. Taken together, the statements about the fear of Yahweh in Proverbs 1 – 9 teach that 'it is wisdom in search of understanding that penetrates everything created, becomes acquainted with it and sees God as the Creator of it all' (Nel 1982: 101). As Proverbs 1:7 states, apart from this fundamental commitment to reverence for Yahweh there is only folly, for fools despise the wisdom and instruction that are derived only from him.

The fear of Yahweh produces a new way of looking at all of life, for it 'sees each moment as the Lord's time, each relationship as the Lord's opportunity, each duty as the Lord's command, and each blessing as the Lord's gift' (Hubbard 1989: 48). This reverence for Yahweh orientates a person to the kind of moral life that corresponds to the creator's values. As Yahweh is just in his character and conduct, so his justice becomes the standard for measuring right and wrong in the realm of human behaviour. The fear of Yahweh represents the desire to please him in all things by respecting the divine order he has constructed in the world (Clements 1992: 62).

Only this kind of transcendent value could truly motivate humans to virtue across the full range of their activities and attitudes. Not only does the fear of Yahweh direct toward positive righteousness, but it also produces hatred of evil (Pr. 3:7b; 8:13). Consequently, all relativistic value systems are rejected by wisdom as inferior because they fail to honour as absolute Yahweh's just order in the world (Brongers 1948: 164; Zornberg 1982: 32).

Conclusion

The worldview of Proverbs 1 – 9 is constructed on four prominent assumptions. First, the universe is Yahweh's creation. Yahweh is not a limited deity as in polytheistic religions, but he is the sole God who has created the entire world. He fashioned the world by his wisdom and understanding, so it is not random and meaningless, but it demonstrates intelligent design. Yahweh's singular creation implies that all of the universe is ultimately dependent upon him. Consequently, there is no dichotomy between sacred and secular spheres of life in the worldview of wisdom. All of life is viewed in terms of its relationship with the creator.

Second, Yahweh is sovereignly controlling the world which he created. This divine order produces a significant degree of predictability between acts and consequences, because the righteous character of Yahweh provides moral governance to the universe. Wisdom seeks to discover the order which Yahweh has embedded in the universe by observing both the physical world and human behaviour. The wise person is skilful in living according to Yahweh's order, but the foolish person diverges from it. Order, however, does not imply deistic mechanism or fatalistic determinism, because Yahweh personally directs the universe which he created.

Third, Yahweh's world is knowable, but it is also mysterious in part. Wisdom is offered to all humans, but only those who fervently seek it will find it. Through observation of life and reception of tradition as transmitted through parents and teachers, one can understand how Yahweh's moral order typically functions in the world. Nevertheless, Yahweh has chosen to leave some of life inscrutable to humans. This sense of mystery is not intended to undermine faith, but to impel humans to faith in the creator who alone comprehends life thoroughly.

Fourth, humans must reverence Yahweh in their lives. The fear of Yahweh is the beginning point for wisdom and knowledge. Every facet of life has a religious dimension, so humans should submit in humble awe as servants to Yahweh. In the worldview of Proverbs 1 – 9 faith seeks understanding, because reverence for Yahweh cultivates the kind of life that mirrors the creator's values.

Chapter Two

Values for education

Every person and every society must make choices between what is bad and what is good, and between what is good and what is best. Choices such as these are made on the basis of perceived values. It is evident that different individuals and different groups make choices that reflect diverse value hierarchies. For example, one family may rear its children to be independent, emphasizing from an early age the importance of making decisions and living with the consequences. On the other hand, another family may stress family solidarity, with the attendant emphasis on the extended family with its complex network of relationships.

The worldview of an individual or a society shapes the values that the person or group holds. Those values, in turn, determine how actions, attitudes, motivations and decisions are evaluated. Because of this, the ethical statements that comprise Proverbs 1 – 9 reflect the religious values of ancient Israel. Just as a person's real values in life can be measured by how he or she uses time and money, so the implicit values of biblical wisdom can be discerned by observing what is praised and what is condemned in the sapiential texts.

Because proverbs draw heavily on observation and tradition, they tend to be useful indicators of the values of a society. Crenshaw reasons:

> It follows that proverbs comprise the best single source for discovering cherished values in ancient Israel. In these succinct sayings we shall come upon deeply rooted ways of life; indeed, we shall even go a long way toward fathoming the people's understanding of good and evil (1981a: 69).

For example, Proverbs 3:14–15 declares that wisdom is better than silver, gold and jewels. In fact, nothing that is commonly

41

desired by humans compares with her. This statement reflects the value judgment that wisdom is superior to material wealth.

It could be argued that proverbial sayings reflect necessarily only the values of their writers or collectors, and not of the society at large. The use of rhetorical questions in Proverbs 1 – 9, however, implies an argument from societal consensus (see chapter 5, pages 119–121). Thus, it is plausible to conclude that the values observable in Proverbs 1 – 9 transcend the personal values of the teacher.

Many scholars have noted the similarities between biblical proverbs and the wisdom literature of ancient Egypt. The parallels are so detailed that it seems scarcely beyond doubt that some form of literary borrowing has taken place. What is not so frequently noted, however, is that though there is significant similarity at the surface level of the language, there is remarkable divergence at the deeper level of values.

McKane (1970: 53–57) argues well that the instructions in Egypt were designed as a vocational manual to develop skill in government service. The ethos of the Egyptian state as a static, ordered society produced a value structure which fostered judicious, reasonable and temperate behaviour. Consequently, moral questions of good and evil were not at the fore of the Egyptian pedagogy.

By contrast, Israel's worldview produced values that brought moral questions to the forefront across the full range of behaviour. For example, whereas in Egypt sexual restraint might be advised because it would assist a person in keeping his government career on track, in Israel sexual purity is evidence of reverence for Yahweh. Certainly the potential for personal harm is also raised as a supportive rationale, but sexual restraint is presented primarily as a matter of righteousness rather than as a matter of prudence.

Just as Israel's values differed from those of its own ancient contemporaries, so they are also distinctive from the values that drive the modern world. To understand the philosophy of education that is implicit in Proverbs 1 – 9, one must discern the key values that wisdom sought to inculcate. In other words, what attitudes and commitments were the pre-eminent concerns of the author? What this text says about the goals and curriculum for education, the process of instruction, and the roles of the teacher and learner all emerges out of the values that it holds.

Wisdom

It is evident from Proverbs 4:5–7 that wisdom is placed as the prime value in life. The teacher charges his student:

> Get wisdom, get understanding;
>> do not forget my words or swerve from them.
> Do not forsake wisdom, and she will protect you;
>> love her, and she will watch over you.
> Wisdom is supreme; therefore get wisdom.
> Though it cost all you have, get understanding.

The final line of this passage has the sense of 'at the price of all you possess'. As McKane comments,

> Wisdom is an unquestionable first in any order of priorities. She should determine the structure of a man's life, giving it form and proportion and establishing a scale of priorities and a right distribution of emphasis (1970: 305).

The Hebrew concept of wisdom (*ḥokmâ*) refers to what is skilful, well made or well judged (Kidner 1964: 13). Though wisdom was used to speak of skill in technical work (Ex. 28:3), in government administration (Dt. 1:13), and in shrewd counsel (2 Sa. 13:3),[1] in the wisdom literature it is most frequently used in the moral sense of skill in living within the moral order of Yahweh's world. In this sense, wisdom 'becomes the fruit of the unending quest for the meaning of man's experience of life and religion' (Scott 1965: xviii).

Wisdom transcends human intelligence and cleverness, for it is rooted in trust in Yahweh. The antithetical parallelism in Proverbs 3:7 makes it explicit that wisdom cannot be found in doing what merely appears to be wise to the individual, but rather in fearing Yahweh and shunning evil. As Proverbs 9:10 concludes, the fear of Yahweh is the beginning of wisdom. Consequently, wisdom requires humble trust in Yahweh, rather than proud self-confidence (von Rad 1972: 102). Wisdom

---

[1] Blank (1962b: 856) details the semantic range of *ḥokmâ* in the Old Testament.

acknowledges the limitations of human understanding, and places its confidence in Yahweh who alone understands exhaustively the world which he created.

Because wisdom is the primary value, it must be loved and sought. The exhortation in Proverbs 7:4 to regard wisdom as a sister and understanding as an intimate friend may well parallel the use of 'sister' in Song of Songs 4:9–10 and the related term 'friend' in Song of Songs 5:16 to refer to intimate love in marriage.

The person who finds wisdom is amply blessed. Wisdom in itself is better than all material things which can be desired (Pr. 8:11). When it is placed first in priority, however, it brings with it many other attendant blessings (Pr. 3:13–18; cf. 1 Ki. 3:5–14). As McKane notes,

> . . . these are the gifts of life in its quantitative and qualitative aspects, length of days, harmonious self-fulfilment, wealth and honour. Only it is the pursuit of Wisdom which brings wealth and so an order of priorities is established. Wisdom is to be sought first and the other things will be added (1970: 295).

Wisdom is frequently contrasted with folly. For example, Proverbs 1:7 states that fools despise wisdom and instruction. Instead of placing as their primary priority in life the pursuit of skill in living as Yahweh intends, fools despise his way as worthless and contemptible (Ross 1991: 907). Folly, then, is not regarded in Proverbs as intellectual deficiency, but inability or unwillingness to conform to Yahweh's order (von Rad 1972: 64). In reality, it is apostasy from the fear of Yahweh (Pr. 1:29) which leads to destruction (1:32). Commenting on these verses, Aitken remarks:

> The fools have had ample warning and ample opportunity to wise up and turn to Lady Wisdom's counsel. But they have chosen to turn away instead, smugly satisfied with themselves and thinking that they know better. Little do they realize, however, that they are bent on suicide (1986: 25).

The fool insists on directing his own life, demanding

autonomy at all costs. Even though it means eventual destruction, the fool makes personal freedom the chief value in life. On the other hand, wisdom chooses to seek what is best in Yahweh's ordered creation. By reverencing Yahweh, the wise person finds skill in living within his world. It is the person who finds wisdom and who gains understanding who is blessed (Pr. 3:13).

Teachability

In addition to valuing wisdom instead of autonomy, Proverbs 1 – 9 regards teachability as a crucial value for life. The section evidences the value of teachability negatively by castigating the rejection of instruction as folly, and positively by demonstrating that the wise person has a teachable spirit.

Numerous verses depict the foolish person as one who rejects instruction. For example, wisdom justifies her lack of support for the foolish because of their refusal to accept her counsel and their resistance to her reproof (Pr. 1:25, 30).

In Proverbs 3:11, the son is charged, '. . . do not despise the LORD's discipline and do not resent his rebuke . . .' This resistance to Yahweh's instruction is the opposite of trusting Yahweh with all the heart, which is exhorted in Proverbs 3:5. Discipline and reproof constitute the dark side of Yahweh's parental love, the painful experiences which can stretch faith to the point of breaking (Aitken 1986: 43). Those who are foolish resent what Yahweh is doing to them, but those who are wise recognize that Yahweh's reproof is evidence of his love and delight for them (Pr. 3:12; cf. Heb. 12:5–11).[2]

It is clear from Proverbs 8:36 that the choice to reject instruction has calamitous consequences, for the one who sins against wisdom injures himself, and all those who hate wisdom love death. Echoing Joshua's charge to Israel (Jos. 24:15),

---

[2] Whybray (1994b: 64) sets this passage in its larger biblical context: 'The problem to which these verses attempt a solution is one which is frequently raised elsewhere in the Old Testament, especially in the Book of Job and in some of the psalms of lamentation; and various solutions are proposed there. The solution offered here is also found elsewhere, the most striking parallel to these verses being Job 5:17–18, whose wording is so similar that some commentators have suggested that one passage influenced the other, although there is no agreement about the chronological priority. But it is also found in such works as Ps. 119, especially vv. 71 and 75.'

'Wisdom insists that we must choose either one path or the other' (Farmer 1991: 56). NIV reflects the contrast with 'whoever *finds* me finds life' in the previous verse by rendering Proverbs 8:36a as 'whoever *fails to find* me'. This also reflects the underlying meaning of the verb *ḥāṭāʾ* (Cohen 1952: 51; Whybray 1994b: 140).

Proverbs 5:22-23 concludes a stern warning against promiscuity with this threat:

> The evil deeds of a wicked man ensnare him;
>   the cords of his sin hold him fast.
> He will die for lack of discipline,
>   led astray by his own great folly.

In his folly the young man rejects instruction. Instead of following the path of wisdom and righteousness, he chooses the way of wickedness. This unfortunate choice will lead to his enslavement.[3]

Rejection of instruction is a degenerative condition that leads to scoffing and folly. Just as Psalm 1:1 warns against the potential harm from walking in the counsel of the wicked, standing in the way of sinners, and sitting in the seat of mockers, so Proverbs 1:22 appeals to three types of people.[4] The simple love their simple ways, because they do not possess the knowledge necessary to make wise decisions. They are easily swayed by temptations because they have not yet developed a strong moral foundation for life.

Mockers disdain wisdom because they take pleasure in tearing down what they do not accept. According to Proverbs 9:7-8, the

---

[3] Aitken (1986: 66) discusses the interesting and plausible rendering of the NEB, which adds special poignancy to the warning in Proverbs 5:23: 'If we follow the New English Bible in verse 23, this foolish man weaves more than the tangled web which traps him; he also weaves his funeral shroud: "he will perish for want of discipline, wrapped in the shroud of his boundless folly". The word "wrapped in the shroud" . . . is the same word the RSV translates "infatuated" in verses 19 and 20, but which the New English Bible renders "wrapped". So it appears that the sage makes a play on this word as the key word to underline and drive home the lesson to be learned: wrap up well in the love of your wife (v. 19) and don't become wrapped up with loose women (v. 20), for that is as good as wrapping yourself in a funeral shroud (v. 23).'

[4] Plaut (1961: 38), Zornberg (1982: 18) and Ross (1991: 910) all give helpful distinctions between the three groups addressed in Proverbs 1:22.

mocker is unteachable, because he rejects both the teacher and the teaching. Instead of welcoming instruction, as do the wise and righteous (9:9), the mocker arrogantly ridicules and rejects teaching, because of his own supposed superiority.[5] By nature, the mocker is 'malicious and impervious to correction or instruction' (Whybray 1994b: 145).

The mocker may regard himself as beyond good and evil, but he will have to face the consequences of the choices he makes. As Proverbs 9:12b states, '. . . if you are a mocker, you alone will suffer.' The stubborn pride of the mocker which makes him reject the instruction of wisdom will cause him to reap the penalty which will ultimately come to him. As McKane remarks well:

> He has become this kind of man through his own obdurate pride in the most private sector of his life and it is there in his loneliness that he must endure the consequences on his personality as they work themselves out inexorably (1970: 369).

The third type of person addressed in Proverbs 1:22 is the fool. The foolish person is one who has settled into a fixed pattern of life in antagonism toward Yahweh's way of wisdom. Instead of welcoming instruction, the fool hates knowledge. Fools despise wisdom and discipline (1:7b), the precise antithesis of the fear of Yahweh, which is the beginning of knowledge (1:7a).

In contrast to the fool's rejection of instruction, the wise person has a teachable spirit. The root of teachability is the fear of Yahweh (Pr. 9:10). To become wise one must begin with a vital relationship with the Lord, an attitude of reverential submission to him which leads the person to accept what he teaches as reliable instruction. Proverbs insists that 'religious devotion constitutes the beginning and fundamental principle of all knowledge' (Crenshaw 1981a: 95).

In addition, the wise person heeds the instruction of teachers. Proverbs 1 – 9 repeatedly uses the expressions 'father' and 'son' to speak of the teacher-pupil relationship (see chapter 4, page

---

[5] McKane (1970: 368–369) notes that the mocker is a stock character in the Egyptian Instruction literature as well.

95). In Proverbs 1:8 and 6:20, however, the explicit reference to the mother lends strong support to a literal family context being in view in these verses. As Whybray (1994b: 37) states, the role of the mother in teaching as a complement to the instruction of the father is unique to Israel among the ancient wisdom traditions, for it is not attested in the parallel Egyptian and Babylonian texts. To be wise, the child must heed the instructions and direction received at home. Their teaching 'will prove a reliable guide, a watchful guard, and an agreeable companion' (Aitken 1986: 69, commenting on Pr. 6:20–22).

Moreover, the teachable person learns from past tradition. Rather than demanding the right to learn solely from personal experience, an approach to life fraught with risk, he acquires wise counsel from those who have preceded him. Eschewing total independence of judgment, the wise person learns as well from the accumulated insights of others. McKane (1970: 266) observes:

> . . . no man can be wise who has not steeped himself in that wisdom which is the deposit of the best minds of many generations. There is a strong sense of the continuity of tradition and of its organic character. The apprentice sage does not remain outside it, confronting it as an external body of knowledge, but he appropriates it in such a way that it becomes part of himself and makes him the kind of person he is, shaping his attitudes and controlling his judgements.

Two implications flow from this acceptance of past tradition. Wisdom is firmly committed to lifelong learning, for as Proverbs 9:9 states, 'Instruct a wise man and he will be wiser still; teach a righteous man and he will add to his learning.' By remaining teachable, even in the adult years, the wise person continues to grow in the understanding of life in Yahweh's world. Furthermore, learning from the past provides a solid foundation for personal choices in the present. The approach of Proverbs 1 – 9 may be summarized as follows: '*First* achieve expertise, and *then* when you go through life you may do things your own way and be effective' (Cox 1982b: 100).

Righteousness

The third value that is a salient concern in Proverbs 1 – 9 is righteousness. This value is affirmed both by negative descriptions of the foolish person who seeks what is evil, and by positive statements regarding the commitment of wisdom to righteousness.

In Proverbs 2 the learner is exhorted to seek diligently for wisdom, for when wisdom enters into his heart it will guard him against the inverted values of folly (2:12–15). Wisdom provides the necessary perspective to protect the learner from the evil one who 'deserts straight roads in preference for those paths and tracks which twist and turn' (McKane 1970: 284). Instead of submitting to the way which Yahweh has ordered in his world, the foolish person leaves what is righteous because he delights in doing what is evil.

Proverbs 6:12–15 and 6:16–19[6] contain two complementary descriptions of the kinds of actions and attitudes which Yahweh hates and judges. Like the society of Noah's day, when every inclination of human hearts was only evil all the time (Gn. 6:5), so the wicked person has a life given to evil ends. In speech, gestures, purposes and actions this life is perverse, for it veers away from Yahweh's ordained path for life.

This deeply rooted commitment to evil destroys both the individual who sins (Pr. 6:15) and the whole basis for communal life (6:19). McKane observes insightfully:

> Whether it be in the abuse of inventiveness for evil ends, or in the contempt for law and the rights of others, or in lying (particularly perjury), these are men who employ their talents in order to destroy the basis

[6] Whybray (1994b: 99–100) elaborates on the significance of using a numerical sequence to define how the universe works: 'Characteristic of the numerical proverb is that it does not merely set out a list of items side by side without overtly specifying their common features, but in a (usually) introductory statement specifies that these are linked by such a common feature (here that they are hateful to Yahweh) and states how many such items there are. This type of saying is not restricted to the Old Testament, but is found among a variety of peoples including the Babylonians, Indians, Arabs and Greeks, and also occurs in post-biblical Jewish literature. Such lists are believed to constitute early attempts to understand the principles of order in the universe, including human nature and society, by classification and enumeration.'

of common life. What is described is a deep-seated corruption of motives which gives rise to a constant and dedicated malevolence tantamount to a total incapacity for neighbourliness. When such chronic bad will is allied with resourcefulness, thoroughness and deceit, it assumes its most dangerous shape and wreaks havoc in a community (1970: 326).

As Proverbs 14:34 declares, righteousness exalts a nation, but sin is a disgrace to any people. Commitment to evil destroys the fabric of social life.

In Proverbs 4:14–17 the teacher warns the learner not to enter the path of the wicked, because evil is addictive. In contrast to Proverbs 3:24, which promises sweet sleep to the one who keeps sound judgment and discernment (3:21), the wicked 'cannot sleep till they do evil; they are robbed of slumber till they make someone fall' (4:16). In fact, their food and drink are wickedness (4:17), for evil dominates their lives. By using this image the teacher emphasizes as strongly as possible that 'choosing the wrong road inevitably leads to a total deterioration of character' (Whybray 1994b: 80).

From the first chapter of Proverbs onwards the teacher cautions his student against those who are wicked. In Proverbs 1:10–19 he states two reasons why the son should avoid them: their actions are both evil (1:16)[7] and short-sighted (1:17–19). To follow in the way of sinners is foolish, because they abandon the righteous law of Yahweh, and they will eventually be destroyed by the lifestyle to which they have become addicted.

In contrast to the foolish person who seeks what is evil, wisdom is committed to righteousness. Wisdom declares in Proverbs 8:13[8] that to fear Yahweh is to hate evil in all of its

[7] Whybray (1994b: 41) argues that Pr. 1:16, which is virtually identical with Is. 59:7a and is lacking in the best manuscripts of the LXX, should be viewed as a gloss. His argument that the motive clause in 1:17–19 more appropriately follows v. 15 is plausible, but v. 16 adds a theological rationale for avoiding the sinners which certainly is suitable in terms of the values which dominate Proverbs 1 – 9.

[8] Whybray (1994b: 124) may well be right in concluding that this verse is a gloss representing a commonplace of the wisdom literature, such as Pr.16:6. On the other hand, the similar wording in 3:7b demonstrates that in Pr. 1 – 9 reverence for Yahweh is viewed in terms of rejection of evil.

forms. Because Yahweh is righteous, reverence for him necessarily entails both embracing what is righteous and rejecting what is unrighteous. Consequently, all that is evil, whether it be an arrogant attitude, sinful actions or perverted speech, lies outside the bounds of wisdom. Proverbs insists on the integrated life, in which the whole person is characterized by righteousness, not a bifurcated life in which righteousness and evil co-exist as an unstable antithesis. Cohen comments:

> Whereas in practice men combine a worship of God with the performance of unethical deeds, wisdom insists that His service, when rightly apprehended, is impossible without the rejection and abhorrence of all that can be classified as evil (1952: 46).

It is clear from Proverbs 2:6–9 that wisdom is more than just an intellectual attainment. The language in this passage is replete with moral terms, such as 'upright', 'blameless', 'just' and 'faithful'. As McKane asserts, '. . . the moralism of the passage is reflected in its vocabulary, and the effect of this is to equate wisdom and unwisdom with good and evil, justice and injustice, uprightness and perversity, righteousness and unrighteousness' (1970: 282). Yahweh's gift of wisdom (2:6) to those who are upright (2:7) enables them to discern what is right, just and fair (2:9).

The qualities listed in Proverbs 2:9 strongly parallel the purpose statement in the prologue of the book (1:3b). 'Right' speaks of conformity to a standard (*cf.* Dt. 25:15). In this context it refers to what is right according to the standard of the law of Yahweh (Ross 1991: 905). The term 'justice' is often joined with righteousness (*cf.* Ps. 106:3) to indicate 'the kind of conduct toward others which God requires of his people' (Whybray 1994b: 33). 'Fair' (*cf.* Pr. 8:6) indicates words or actions that are honest and truthful. Each of the terms in Proverbs 1:3b evaluates actions on the basis of how they correspond to a fixed standard of right established by Yahweh. The measure for behaviour is not subjective personal desire, relative cultural norms, or the pragmatic test of what works, but rather how well it corresponds to Yahweh's righteous standard.

This commitment to Yahweh's objective standard of righteousness is confirmed by the speech of wisdom in Proverbs

8:6–9. There is nothing crooked or perverted in what wisdom says, for her mouth utters truth and righteousness. As Whybray (1994b: 123) notes, these terms 'are both frequently used in the Old Testament of God and of those who conform their conduct to his standards'. Wisdom appeals to those who are simple and foolish (8:5) to discern in her righteous teachings that which corresponds to Yahweh's way.

Not only is righteousness the proper focus for the individual, but it is also the foundation for just government. Wisdom declares in Proverbs 8:15–16:

> By me kings reign
>   and rulers make laws that are just;
> by me princes govern,
>   and all nobles who rule on earth.[9]

This claim is supported by other witnesses in the larger wisdom tradition, such as Proverbs 29:4: 'By justice a king gives a country stability, but one who is greedy for bribes tears it down.'[10] Contrary to ideologies which equate law with the will of the monarch or even the will of the people, Proverbs 1 – 9, in agreement with what the Bible generally affirms, holds that Yahweh's righteous standard is the absolute measure by which all human governments must be judged. Wisdom, then, is committed to righteousness at every level of life, from personal behaviour to governmental rule.

Life

Proverbs 1 – 9, in keeping with the emphasis of the entire biblical wisdom corpus, places high value upon life. Life, however, is not mere physical existence, but it is viewed as substantial, meaningful existence within Yahweh's ordered boundaries. In recommending genuine life, the wisdom teacher contrasts it with the counterfeits that only purport to give life.

[9] Cohen (1952: 46) argues unconvincingly that the final word of Pr. 8:16 should be construed with several Hebrew manuscripts as 'of the earth'. It is more likely that the variant was introduced as a corruption from Is. 40:23 and that the MT reading should be retained.

[10] This commitment to righteousness in political rule is also affirmed in 2 Sa. 23:3–4; Pss. 72, 101.

The wise person values genuine life in its substantial qualities, but the foolish person is attracted to and destroyed by superficial pleasures that only appear to make life meaningful.

Proverbs 1:10–19 warns against the temptation to place the acquisition of money above doing what is right. In this passage the young man is invited by his peers to get riches through a career in crime. They promise him an equal share in the venture (1:14), which they claim will be highly profitable (1:13).

The teacher, however, strips the mask off their deception. Far from giving life, the pursuit of money by illegal means leads to death. Proverbs 1:18–19 states:

> These men lie in wait for their own blood;
>> they waylay only themselves!
> Such is the end of all who go after their ill-gotten gain;
>> it takes away the lives of those who get it.

As will be seen, one of the blessings in life which wisdom gives is prosperity, but

> ... wealth gained at the expense of wisdom is poisonous fruit; there is no short cut to success, for wealth is worthless unless it is a measure of the intrinsic worth of its possessor. It is right that the wise man should be prosperous, but this route by way of lawlessness, cupidity and violence leads to death (McKane 1970: 269).

In addition to money wrongfully acquired, the foolish person is also attracted by leisure. Once again, wisdom does promise peace and security, but the craving for leisure which results in indolence and laziness leads to poverty. After the teacher points to the example of the industrious ant (Pr. 6:6–8), he calls the sluggard to task in 6:9–11:

> How long will you lie there, you sluggard?
>> When will you get up from your sleep?
> A little sleep, a little slumber,
>> a little folding of the hands to rest –
> and poverty will come on you like a bandit
> and scarcity like an armed man.

In avoiding work, making excuses and deceiving himself, the sluggard is unable to face challenges as they arise. His desire for the good and easy life leaves him defenceless before destitution. Alden (1983: 57) remarks insightfully: 'In a sense he robs himself by wasting away his time, talents, and earning power. Precious hours, important opportunities, and years of productivity are squandered because he lacks enthusiasm and initiative.' In valuing leisure above diligence, the sluggard forfeits what he has and what he could have.

The predominant superficial pleasure against which the young man is warned is illicit sex (Pr. 2:16–19; 5:3–23; 6:24–35; 7:5–27; 9:13–18). There has been extensive debate regarding the identity of the strange or foreign woman who appears frequently in Proverbs 1 – 9. Cohen (1952: 11) draws on the wider biblical context with its reproofs against adultery and warnings against foreign women and supports a literal rendering. McKane (1970: 284–286) agrees in the main with the literal interpretation, pointing to analogous warnings in the Egyptian Instructions against affairs with women, but he construes 'foreign' as being outside the boundaries of the law and the culture. As McKane sees it, '. . . she defies religious and social sanctions and conventions and is a law to herself. As such she is particularly deadly to young men who become embroiled with her' (1970: 285).

On the other hand, the reference to the strange woman is often viewed in religious terms as a solicitation to evil and folly. The term zārâ can be used for religious infidelity, as for example when Israel worshipped strange gods (Dt. 32:16; Ps. 81:9[10]). As Farmer (1991: 33) notes, in Proverbs 2:17b the woman is described as forgetting the covenant of her God.

Additional support for the religious connotation of foreignness comes from Ross (1991: 914), who points to the fact that the strange woman offers communion sacrifices (Pr. 7:14), which identifies her most likely as an Israelite. In Ross's view, 'the term does not necessarily mean that she is a foreigner; rather she is estranged from the corporate life of the community with its social and religious conventions . . . Such a woman is acting outside the legal bounds of marriage within the covenant.'

In the total structure of Proverbs 1 – 9 the learner, a young man, is presented with two contrasting alternatives. Wisdom makes her appeal in Proverbs 1:20–33 and 8:1–36. The young man is warned against the invitation of the strange or foreign woman in Proverbs 2:16–19; 5:3–23; 6:24–35; and 7:5–27. In the final chapter of the section, the two women representing wisdom (9:1–6) and folly (9:13–18) are juxtaposed as they address the young man with nearly identical language.

For young men, illicit sex is an alluring temptation to be avoided, and the explicit language by which the strange woman invites him should not be discounted. It is likely that a literal warning against sexual seduction is in view in these passages, particularly in light of her graphic enticements, including the long absence of her husband (7:16–20). In addition, the teacher counsels the young man to rejoice in the wife of his youth, finding satisfaction in physical intimacy with her (5:15–20).

At the same time, the Old Testament frequently speaks of religious apostasy as adultery (cf. Ho. 1 – 3), certainly because it entails alienation of proper affection for Yahweh, and probably because cultic prostitution was a stock element in foreign religions such as Baalism. Consequently, it is appropriate to view the image of the strange or foreign woman in Proverbs 1 – 9 as functioning at both the literal and the metaphorical levels. Although the warning against illicit sex is a crucial caution for the learner, 'this portrait of the *femme fatale* also stands for the allure of foreign cults and therefore warns against *religious* infidelity' (Blenkinsopp 1983: 136).

Just as wisdom delivers the learner from the evil man who leaves the paths of righteousness (Pr. 2:12–15), so it also delivers him from the allurements of the strange woman who flatters with her words (2:16–19). Though what she says is appealing, those who follow her find to their regret that her path leads to death:

> For her house leads down to death
> and her paths to the spirits of the dead.[11]

---

[11] McKane (1970: 287–288) draws upon the Ugaritic literature to interpret the significance of the term $r^e p\bar{a}$'$\hat{i}m$ in this passage: 'I would suggest that the verse contains two Canaanite mythological allusions. The first half alludes to the god Mot, whose gaping throat is the gateway to Sheol, and the second half alludes either to the gods of that underworld (the Ugaritic *rpum*) or to the massed community of the world of the dead. The estranged woman, the outsider, lives on the borders of the land of the dead and her paths descend towards the $r^e p\bar{a}$'$\hat{i}m$. What does this metaphor mean? It is a warning that those

None who go to her return
or attain the paths of life (2:18–19).

She promises much delight, but delivers only disappointment.

In Proverbs 5:3–6 the young man is warned especially against the deceitful speech of the woman. Her words drip honey (*cf.* Song 4:11) and they are smoother than oil, because she is 'well practised in the art of seduction' (Aitken 1986: 62). In the end, however, her sweetness turns into the bitterness of wormwood,[12] and her smoothness is replaced by a sharp sword. She offers pleasure, but she leads to pain. In this she is the antithesis to wisdom, for 'just as wisdom's path makes life rich and full and really worth living, and leads to ripeness of age, so the seductress's path impoverishes life and robs it of meaning, and leads in the end to an untimely death' (Aitken 1986: 63).

The warning in Proverbs 6:24–35 places special emphasis on the undesirable consequences of succumbing to the entice-ments of the evil woman, or perhaps better, the neighbour's wife (*cf.* 6:29).[13] Adultery leads to enslavement, just as surely as grasping fire burns one's clothes and walking on hot coals scorches the feet (6:27–28). The short-term satisfaction of sexual desire is purchased at the high price of poverty (6:26), for though resorting to a prostitute may reduce a man to minimal means, sexual entanglement with another man's wife brings total financial and personal ruin (Whybray 1994b: 105). Her jealous husband will see to it that the offender is disgraced

---

who become entangled with such a woman are irrevocably involved with her in her estrangement from society. They, too, will become outcasts and every door will be shut on them, every relationship severed. They will be treated like lepers, and the sentence which society passes on them will be for life.'

[12] Greenstone (1950: 47) observes: 'Wormwood is an aromatic plant, very bitter to the taste, formerly employed to protect clothing and furniture from insects, and used in the Bible to indicate the dire results of sin (Deut. 29.17; Amos 5.7; 6.12; Jer. 9.14; Lam 3.15, 19).'

[13] Farmer (1991: 46) argues reasonably for this alternative reading: 'In 6:24a the translation "evil woman" is possible from the Hebrew (MT), but a very small change in vowel pointing would make the phrase read "neighbor's wife" (as in v. 29). The words are nearly identical here with the commandment "you shall not covet your neighbor's wife" (Exod. 20:17). In fact, the Greek translators of the LXX understood the text in that way (as the NEB reflects in its rendering: "to keep you from the wife of another man"). Since the technical term for committing adultery (*no'eph*) does occur in Prov. 3:32, the Greek text (and the NEB) probably reflect the original sense more accurately.'

(6:33) and vengeance is exacted to the full measure of the law (6:34–35).

The elaborate description in Proverbs 7:6–23 serves as the backdrop for the repeated warnings against the foreign woman in 7:1–5 and 24–27. The teacher pictures a youth being solicited by a woman 'dressed as a harlot and cunning of heart' (7:10). She flatters him by saying that she has made special preparation just for him. She promises a night of sexual pleasure without risk of detection, because her husband has gone on a long journey (7:18–20). The folly of the youth deludes him into accepting her offer, believing that 'he can indulge in an illicit liaison without suffering any consequences' (Farmer 1991: 49). Only too quickly he learns that, like a bird hastening into a snare, so he has chosen the path which will cost him his life (7:23).

Whether the images of the foreigner or stranger in Proverbs 1 – 9 refer to illicit sexual activity or to religious apostasy, they clearly portray the foolishness of living outside the limits of Yahweh's order. As Van Leeuwen notes,

> . . . good means staying within prescribed religio-moral boundaries and evil means the trespassing of these limits. To stay 'in bounds' means life, to go 'out of bounds' entails death. Positive human existence is a life within limits, embracing freedom within form. But walking, living, loving beyond the limits ordained by Wisdom leads to death, like a fish out of water (1990: 116).

In contrast to the foolish person who is attracted to and destroyed by the superficial pleasures of illegal gain, indolent leisure and illicit sex, wisdom values genuine life in its substantial qualities. Thus, the teacher implores the learner in Proverbs 7:1–2:

> My son, keep my words
>   and store up my commands within you.
> Keep my commands and you will live;
>   guard my teachings as the apple of your eye.[14]

[14] Whybray (1994b: 111) gives a helpful explanation of this figure: 'As the context suggests, and as the other occurrences (Dt. 32:10; Ps. 17:8) confirm,

It is clear from this usage that life for the wise teacher is more than mere physical existence. Rather, obedience to the commandments of wisdom leads to life in a fuller, qualitative sense of abounding vitality (McKane 1970: 333).

As Proverbs 4:13 teaches, instruction in wisdom is the key to acquiring life. The focus of this life is not immortality in a future world, but, in keeping with the focus of the wisdom literature in general, 'wisdom is thoroughly oriented to this life and this world, and the enjoyment of wisdom is itself life in the fullest sense' (Collins 1980b: 23). It is true that Proverbs 3:16 speaks of wisdom holding long life in her right hand, but transcending this quantitative notion is the more characteristic notion of wisdom providing life of enduring and satisfying quality. Attaining this kind of life requires a conscious choice to seek it. Not only must the learner walk in the way of understanding (Pr. 9:6b), but he also must leave his simple ways if he is truly to live (9:6a). Finding life, therefore, demands that one choose to forsake the broad path to superficial pleasures which the simple and the foolish crave, and instead set one's course on the narrow road of wisdom which leads eventually and certainly to life. Real life cannot be found unless it is consciously sought.

Proverbs 1 – 9 describes several components of the genuine life which wisdom values. Proverbs 3:18 uses synonymous parallelism to state that wisdom is a tree of life which provides happiness to those who lay hold of her. The image of the tree of life is familiar in biblical literature, harking back to the description of the original paradise in Genesis 2 – 3. Its uses in Proverbs 11:30, 13:12 and 15:4 suggest that it may have become a stock expression in the wisdom tradition for happiness in life. At very least the tree of life represents the vitality which wisdom gives (McKane 1970: 296).[15] In the wider canonical perspective, however, the tree of life speaks of immortality, both in its initial appearance in the Garden of Eden (Gn. 3:22) and in its final appearance in the new

---

this phrase denotes something especially precious, a meaning which has passed into some European languages including English. In a literal sense the "apple" of the eye is the pupil. *'îšôn* is a diminutive form of *'îš*, "a man": one's image reflected in the eye of another person was seen as a "little man" looking out.

[15] Whybray (1994b: 67) argues that 'tree of life' should be rendered 'staff of life'. He reasons that *'ēṣ* is frequently used for wooden objects, particularly for a stick or staff. He fails, however, to analyse adequately the fixed expression 'the tree of life', which has a long and significant history in the biblical text.

Jerusalem (Rev. 22:2). Garrett (1993: 82) may well be right when he claims that separation from the tree of life in Genesis 3:24 meant that humans lost their chance for immortality, but through wisdom there is 'the promise of escape from the curse of death'. Nevertheless, even if the tree of life does have the overtones of immortality, the primary note sounded by the expression is that of genuine happiness in the present life.

Closely related to happiness is the quality of peace promised in Proverbs 3:1–2 to those who keep the commandments of wisdom:

> My son, do not forget my teaching,
>   but keep my commands in your heart,
>   for they will prolong your life many years
>   and bring you prosperity.

The Hebrew word *šālôm* refers to more than absence of hostility. It is a comprehensive term which speaks of wholeness of life, including both security without and serenity within (Greenstone 1950: 25). As Proverbs 3:17 teaches, the ways of wisdom are pleasant ways, and all of her paths are peace, for they lead to genuine contentment and satisfaction in life.

The life which wisdom values is also characterized by security. In contrast to the destruction which fools endure (Pr. 1:32), wisdom promises secure life to those who listen to her (1:33). Instead of dreading calamity,[16] 'those who listen submissively and attentively will live in security and will have their minds set at rest from the terror of evil' (McKane 1970: 276).

Similarly, Proverbs 2:21–22 teach that those who live righteously, according to the dictates of wisdom, will experience security:

> For the upright will live in the land,
>   and the blameless will remain in it;
>   but the wicked will be cut off from the land,
>   and the unfaithful will be torn from it.

---

[16] Whybray (1994b: 49) is correct in noting that *rā'â*, translated in Pr. 1:33 as 'harm', is 'not used in an ethical sense but means harm or misfortune such as is to be the lot of those who ignore Wisdom's teaching according to the previous verses'.

For the people of Israel, living in the land meant secure existence in the land promised by Yahweh to Abraham (Gn. 12:1; 13:13–17; 15:18–21; 17:8). As Israel was poised to begin the conquest of the land, Moses reminded the people in Deuteronomy 30:15–20 that continued possession of the land would be conditional upon their obedience to Yahweh's commandments. He said: 'For I command you today to love the LORD your God, to walk in his ways, and to keep his commands, decrees and laws; then you will live and increase, and the LORD your God will bless you in the land you are entering to possess' (Dt. 30:16). Life in the land, then, is secure existence under the blessing of Yahweh. This security in life is available only for those who follow the path of wisdom in obedience to him.

Wisdom also values a life of prosperity, although here there is a measure of ambivalence in Proverbs 1 – 9. On the one hand, Proverbs 3:14–15 exclaims that wisdom surpasses material wealth:

> For she is more profitable than silver
> and yields better returns than gold.
> She is more precious than rubies;
> nothing you desire can compare with her.

Personified wisdom herself supports this value judgment in Proverbs 8:10–11:

> Choose my instruction instead of silver,
> knowledge rather than choice gold,
> for wisdom is more precious than rubies,
> and nothing you desire can compare with her.

On the other hand, in Proverbs 8:18–21 wisdom also claims that her wealth which surpasses material prosperity includes material riches as well:

> With me are riches and honour,
> enduring wealth and prosperity.
> My fruit is better than fine gold;
> what I yield surpasses choice silver.
> I walk in the way of righteousness,
> along the paths of justice,

bestowing wealth on those who love me
and making their treasuries full.

In other words, wisdom does not view poverty as intrinsically virtuous, or riches as intrinsically corrupt. What is of primary concern is that one should love wisdom (8:21). If that condition is met, then wisdom is not hesitant in endowing those who love her with wealth. In this passage it is evident that

> ... the wealth offered by Wisdom is not to be understood in a figurative sense but is quite literally material wealth which, because it is gained through Wisdom rather than directly as an end in itself, is more worthwhile than gold and silver obtained in the usual way without regard to her (v. 19) because it will be enduring (Whybray 1994b: 126).

The life valued by wisdom is also characterized by honour. Proverbs 3:4 teaches that those who keep kindness and truth 'will win favour and a good name in the sight of God and man.' It is important to note that honour comes both in the vertical dimension of one's relationship with God and in the horizontal dimension of one's relationships within society. The wise person enhances the life of the community, and in turn receives favour from the community (O'Conner 1988: 21). More than that human acclaim, however, the one who finds wisdom 'receives favour from the LORD' (8:35), which is the epitome of life.

Throughout Proverbs 1 – 9 the young man faces the competing alternatives of wisdom and folly, both depicted as women seeking his love. The insistent solicitations by the strange woman lead to dishonour and death (3:35b; *cf.* 5:22–23) for the one who is enticed by her allurements. Wisdom, however, honours those who embrace her (4:8–9):

> Esteem her [wisdom], and she will exalt you;
> embrace her, and she will honour you.
> She will set a garland of grace on your head
> and present you with a crown of splendour.

It is 'by embracing Wisdom that the pathway to advancement, esteem and reputation is opened up' (McKane 1970: 306).

Conclusion

By evaluating what is praised and what is condemned in Proverbs 1 – 9, the implicit values for education can be ascertained. In contrast to the primarily pragmatic values of the Egyptian wisdom literature, Proverbs 1 – 9 reflects a worldview that builds values upon a moral and theological base.

The prime value for life is wisdom, which speaks of skill in living within the moral order of Yahweh's world. Wisdom is rooted in trust in Yahweh, and it provides ample blessings to those who pursue it earnestly. It is the antithesis of folly, which is rejection of Yahweh's order because of one's insistence on personal autonomy.

Proverbs 1 – 9 values teachability, or a humble willingness to accept instruction from Yahweh and from human teachers. Rejection of instruction leads into progressively degenerative forms of folly, which eventually bring one to destruction. By contrast, the teachable person grows continually in the understanding of life within Yahweh's world.

Furthermore, education in Proverbs 1 – 9 is firmly committed to righteousness. Evil in all of its forms is destructive to life, but wisdom grounded in the fear of Yahweh hates evil. Righteousness, or conformity to the law of Yahweh, is the objective standard by which every facet of life is measured. Wisdom is committed to righteousness throughout every dimension of human existence.

Moreover, life as substantial, meaningful existence within Yahweh's ordered boundaries is valued above all counterfeits which promise satisfaction. Illegal gain, indolent leisure and illicit sex are temptations which can allure young men in particular. Genuine life, however, comes from embracing wisdom, for it is the road of wisdom which leads to life. Life, according to Proverbs 1 – 9, encompasses peace, security, prosperity and honour.

Chapter Three

Goals for education

As a teacher constructs a course syllabus or a lesson plan for a class session, she must determine the goals that will be attempted. In pedagogy, goals are often described as cognitive (knowledge), affective (attitudes) and psycho-motor (skills) objectives. The specific goals for the course or class will affect the content which is presented, the mode of instruction, and the role of the teacher and the learner within the learning context.

Proverbs 1 – 9 contains a wealth of information regarding the goals of education in this portion of the biblical wisdom corpus. There are numerous explicit statements indicating the outcomes that the teacher desires to produce in the learner. In addition, frequent implicit indicators help to define the goals of education envisioned in Proverbs 1 – 9.

It is evident that the transmission of knowledge from one generation to the next is an integral part of what education is seeking to accomplish. Knowledge, however, is not viewed as an end in itself, but is only the foundation for more significant goals such as understanding and application.[1] Facts gleaned from personal observation and from tradition are important means to the greater outcomes that the teacher endeavours to achieve. What is paramount is moral behaviour (Fox 1968: 55), not the knowledge that is its substratum.

The programmatic introduction in Proverbs 1:2–7 sets the course for at least Proverbs 1 – 9, and perhaps for the entire book of Proverbs. In this statement of purpose, part of the goal for what is to follow is to give to the youth knowledge (1:4), but

---

[1] This insight has been developed in the seminal study on educational objectives by B. S. Bloom *et al.* (1956). An excellent application of Bloom's theory to classroom teaching is found in N. E. Gronlund (1985).

the clear emphasis is placed on instruction in wisdom. As Perdue observes:

> The purpose of the collection and the larger book is instruction in wisdom, or *mûsār* – that is, knowledge about God, the world, and human life; the embodiment of sapiential piety and virtue; and the construction of a world for human dwelling. The introduction serves as an invitation to pursue the study of wisdom (1994: 78).

The biblical emphasis on wisdom as the primary goal for education contrasts with the pragmatic purposes in Egyptian and Mesopotamian instruction. In those ancient Near Eastern cultures, wisdom was closely linked with the state bureaucracy. The court scribes used instruction to teach the élite youth from prominent families how 'to ensure success in the exercise of governmental responsibilities' (Crenshaw 1993b: 166). In Israel the provenance of wisdom included the court (*cf.* Pr. 25:1; 1 Ki. 4:29–34), but it was also most probably cultivated in the clan and the family. Instead of being the exclusive property of the élite, wisdom in Israel was 'broadly-based instruction for the community and especially for the young men of the community' (McKane 1970: 9).

What is remarkable to note is that the outcomes desired in Proverbs 1 – 9, though expressed in the distinctive language of wisdom, are comparable to the standards in the Mosaic law. Both wisdom and law in the Old Testament share the same worldview, in which Yahweh has created the world and placed within it his order. Consequently, the instructions in Proverbs, just as the legal prescriptions of the covenant, call humans to honour Yahweh through lives characterized by obedience, justice, integrity and compassion (Childs 1979: 558). The special contribution of wisdom is in its challenge to apply the covenant faith to every area of life. In doing this the wisdom teachers 'put heart, feet, hands, and tongue to the conviction that Yahweh, the Creator-Redeemer-Lawgiver-King, was indeed Lord of everyone and everything' (Hubbard 1989: 29).

Commitment

Foundational to all of the goals of education in Proverbs 1 – 9 is the development of the personal commitment of the learner. The teacher does not just seek passive acceptance of the tradition that he transmits, but rather cultivates an active desire by the learner to appropriate wisdom for himself. In other words, a chief goal of education is to reproduce in the life of the learner the values which have been described in chapter 2. This will be accomplished only if the learner becomes an active and enthusiastic participant in the learning process.

Commitment involves diligence, 'the willingness to channel energy into one's responsibilities' (O'Conner 1988: 42). This kind of single-minded attention is encouraged in Proverbs 2:1–4:

> My son, if you accept my words
>> and store up my commands within you,
> turning your ear to wisdom
>> and applying your heart to understanding,
> and if you call out for insight
>> and cry aloud for understanding,
> and if you look for it as for silver
>> and search for it as for hidden treasure . . .

This diligence involves applying the heart (2:2) to understanding, that is, employing the full resources of the reasoning faculty (Greenstone 1950: 16) in seeking for the path of wisdom. It is compared to the painstaking search by miners to locate hidden treasure such as silver. Careless, half-hearted effort does not suffice, for wisdom requires the utmost diligence. As Aitken states well, 'Neither silver ore nor wisdom is got in a day, or got without industry; but for miner and student alike, the prize is worth the toil. But toil there is; and so an earnest desire to obtain wisdom must be uppermost' (1986: 27).

Proverbs 3:3b alludes to Deuteronomy 6:8–9 in exhorting the son to give careful attention to kindness and truth: '. . . bind them around your neck, write them on the tablet of your heart.' Though the Israelites came to apply this instruction literally by wearing phylacteries, the point of the metaphor is that the learner needs to keep the godly values which he has been taught ever fresh in his mind (Cohen 1952: 13). Unlike a student who memorizes facts for an examination only to forget them promptly after the test is past, the learner in Proverbs is challenged to keep the truth ever before him. A similar exhortation is given in Proverbs 6:21 regarding the instructions of parents: 'Bind them upon your heart for ever; fasten them around your neck,' and in Proverbs 8:33–35 a word of blessing is proclaimed on the one who diligently seeks wisdom:

> Listen to my instruction and be wise;
>   do not ignore it.
> Blessed is the man who listens to me,
>   watching daily at my doors,
>   waiting at my doorway.
> For whoever finds me finds life
>   and receives favour from the LORD.

As Whybray (1994b: 139) notes, the Song of Songs, reflecting ancient conventions in love poetry, uses the terms 'seek', 'find' and 'door' to refer to the lover seeking entrance to the house and heart of his beloved. In the same way, only the learner who is diligent in seeking wisdom will enjoy the delights which wisdom longs to bestow.

The goal of personal commitment to wisdom is also manifest in the term *mûsār*, rendered 'instruction' or 'discipline'. Used thirteen times in Proverbs 1 – 9, *mûsār* speaks of life under control. Often this control begins as external restraint, as in Proverbs 3:11; 5:12; 6:23 and 7:22. Ideally, however, the imposed restraints are transformed into internal self-control, as in Proverbs 4:13 and 8:33. This mastery of self is evidenced by control in speech, passions and appetites (Aitken 1986: 11). Ultimately, *mûsār* is respect for Yahweh and his teaching which is demonstrated by the individual's submissive obedience (McKane 1970: 290). Instead of living according to his own preferences, the disciplined learner chooses to keep his life under control by living within the boundaries which Yahweh has established.

In addition to diligence and discipline, commitment is evidenced by devotion to wisdom as the chief object of affection. Wisdom is a valuable object which justifies whatever price one has to pay to acquire it (Pr. 4:7). The same level of commitment, however, must be maintained if wisdom is to be a permanent possession. Proverbs 3:21, therefore, challenges the son to 'preserve sound judgment and discernment' and 'do not let them out of your sight'. Wisdom must be retained at all costs, because careless neglect can cause one to lose it.

Devotion to wisdom is urged most compellingly by using the image of sincere love for a woman. This figure is appropriate in Proverbs, because the learner is envisioned as a young man receiving the instructions of his father. Throughout Proverbs 1 – 9 wisdom and folly are portrayed as women who are rivals for the learner's love. Consequently, 'seeking and finding Wisdom is compared on a human level to finding and embracing a lovely and graceful woman who is the object of the heart's desire' (Perdue 1994: 82; *cf.* Eaton 1989: 87).

Proverbs 7:1–5 demonstrates this call to wholehearted love for wisdom:

> My son, keep my words
>> and store up my commands within you.
> Keep my commands and you will live;
>> guard my teachings as the apple of your eye.
> Bind them on your fingers;
>> write them on the table of your heart.
> Say to wisdom, 'You are my sister,'
>> and call understanding your kinsman;
> they will keep you from the adulteress,
>> from the wayward wife with her seductive words.

Similarly, Wisdom refers to those who love her in Proverbs 8:17, 21. The teacher assures the son, 'Love her [wisdom], and she will watch over you' (4:6), and 'Embrace her, and she will honour you' (4:8). Far more than passive acceptance of tradition, these verses manifest the deep devotion of a lover. Wisdom must fill the mind and change the actions, to be sure, but it must also engage the emotions and stir the will to personal commitment. The learner must not only know what wisdom teaches and do what wisdom commands, but he must also love what wisdom values so that his life is shaped in accordance with Yahweh's desires.

Character

A second key goal of education in Proverbs 1 – 9 is the formation of godly character in the learner. The focus of the instructions is on the development of the inner person, not just on the adoption of a pattern of actions. Commenting upon this section, Fox notes appositely:

> Wisdom is a configuration of character, a compound of knowledge, fears, expectations, and desires that enables one to identify the right path and keep to it. Wisdom means not only knowing but also *wanting* to do what is right and to avoid sin (1994: 243).

More than the Mosaic law, which focuses on external actions, wisdom places emphasis on the formation of the foundational character which produces actions. In other words, education in Proverbs 1 – 9 works from the inside out in cultivating change in the life of the learner, rather than working on external actions with the hope that the inner person might change over time.

According to Proverbs, good character is godly character, because it is based on commitment to Yahweh. Proverbs 2:8 states that Yahweh protects those who guard the paths of justice and he preserves the way of his godly ones. Their lives are oriented by Yahweh's order (*mišpāṭ*), and they are loyal (*ḥāsîd*) to him and his standards.[2] This religious commitment is the bedrock for character, for 'even very basic moral duties are traced back to the adoption of such a right fundamental attitude, which alone can result in a positive and responsible outlook on life' (Clements 1995: 281).

Godly character is the integrating force that unites and directs the entire person. Proverbs 2:7 parallels 'the upright' with 'those whose walk is blameless'. The latter phrase, *hōlᵉkê tōm*, is an expression which is closely related to statements in the narrative and the hymnic literature referring to individuals who are wholehearted in their commitment to Yahweh. For example, in

---

[2] McKane (1970: 283) notes well: 'This verse (v. 8) . . . is controlled by presuppositions of Yahwistic faith and practice. The *ḥāsîd* is the loyal man in a community whose cement is *ḥesed*, a reciprocal loyalty, and the "paths of justice" have been charted by Yahweh for the right ordering of common life.'

Genesis 17:1 Abram is charged by Yahweh, 'Walk before me and be blameless [*tāmîm*].' In 1 Kings 9:4 Yahweh promises to establish the throne of Solomon over Israel for ever if he would walk before Yahweh as his father David walked, in integrity (*tom*) of heart and uprightness. The psalmist asserts that both his past actions (Ps. 26:1) and his future actions (Ps. 26:11) are characterized as walking in blamelessness (*tom*). Furthermore, walking in blamelessness (*tāmîm*) is required for those who abide in the tent of Yahweh (Ps. 15:1[2]) and for those who are recipients of his blessing (Ps. 84:11[12]). Blamelessness, or integrity, speaks of completeness, a wholehearted allegiance to Yahweh which flavours every aspect of life.

In Proverbs 4:23 this emphasis on the entire person is expressed in terms of the heart: 'Above all else, guard your heart, for it is the wellspring of life.' The Hebrews viewed the heart as the centre of the rational and emotional life (Farmer 1991: 40). Because the heart controls all of life, it is the key to personal success or failure. Consequently, the teacher challenges the son to guard it carefully, lest his whole life be ruined. The heart, representative of the character, inevitably affects the outcome of the total person.

The emphasis in Proverbs on the development of character is really a call to growth in maturity as a godly individual. Underlying the recurrent instructions regarding skill in living in the various spheres of life is the need for an increasingly solid foundation of character. To function well in personal disciplines, in interpersonal relationships, in the family, at work, and within the community, growing maturity is essential. Wisdom 'is not concerned primarily with the acquisition and development of professional skills; it is concerned with the development of that moral maturity with which professional skills may be competently utilized' (Craigie 1979: 8).

Good and growing character provides the impetus for lifelong learning, because it is a predisposition to increased wisdom. As Proverbs 9:9 observes,

> Instruct a wise man and he will be wiser still;
> teach a righteous man and he will add to his learning.

The goal of education is not just to transmit a body of facts, but it is to develop in the learner the kind of character that will continually impel him to keep learning and growing. Perdue notes well that:

> ... becoming wise is a way of life, a process that continues for a lifetime, as the wise person seeks to live in harmony with God, the cosmos, the social order, and a human nature, which requires the discipline and structure of teaching (1994: 74).

Competence

A third major goal for education in Proverbs 1 – 9 is the competence of the learner. Unlike the Greek conception of education, which valued knowledge as intrinsically virtuous, the Hebrew wisdom tradition taught knowledge as a means to understand life. Education, then, sought to inculcate the ability to perceive reality and to adjust conduct accordingly (Duhaime 1980: 193). As O'Conner (1988: 31) notes, knowledge 'was directly useful in helping one to understand the created world and to cope with human existence. The more one knew, the better one would be able to live.' This goal of competence in living is seen particularly in seven Hebrew terms featured in Proverbs 1 – 9.

The term 'ormâ, translated 'prudence', occurs three times (Pr. 1:4; 8:5, 12). It involves shrewdness, either in the evil sense of the crafty scheming employed by the serpent in Genesis 3:1, or in the positive sense of foreseeing challenges and making appropriate preparation (cf. 22:3). Prudence is a thoughtful, critical capacity which makes wise discriminations (Zornberg 1982: 75). Because it weighs the consequences before acting, it provides a safeguard against the youthful propensity of being misled by attractive persuasions (Zornberg 1982: 78; Plaut 1961: 30–31).

'Discretion' (m^ezimmâ) is used five times in the section (1:4; 2:11; 3:21; 5:2; 8:12). It speaks of the ability to form plans, or 'the capacity of well-considered action' (Delitzsch 1971: 79). Discretion comes through 'penetrating analyses of ethics that lead to a clear and full comprehension of the principles of the moral law' (Zornberg 1982: 78). In contrast to secular savoir-faire, and also the perversion of discretion into evil craftiness (cf. Jb. 21:27; Pss. 10:2, 4; 21:12) discretion in its proper form finds its source in the divine wisdom (Pr. 8:12). It is, however, not removed from practical life, but views worldly affairs in terms of their moral dimensions. This skill, learned by listening to the teacher (5:1–2), enables one to be resourceful (McKane 1970: 265, 283–284), able carefully to think out plans for action. As Fox observes, '. . . it allows you to think for yourself and to keep your own counsel. When sinners try to seduce you to their ways, you will be able to look inward, think independently, and resist their inveiglements' (Fox 1994: 240).

'Guidance' (*taḥbulâ*), used only in Proverbs 1:5, is drawn from the language of navigation. As von Rad (1962: 421) notes, it refers to the art of steering through the confusion of life, and the individual proverbs in the collection 'resemble buoys set out on the sea by which one can find one's position'. Proverbs 11:14 illustrates this negatively: 'For lack of guidance [*taḥbulōt*] a nation falls, but many advisers make victory sure.' This expertise equips the learner with 'the ability to pick one's way without putting a foot wrong through a confused and tangled situation' (McKane 1970: 266). Through *taḥbulâ* he can think through a problem, determine the best course of response, and steer successfully according to the plan.

By 'sound judgment' (*tûšîyyâ*), a term found three times (2:7; 3:21; 8:14), the idea of effectiveness in getting results is highlighted (Aitken 1986: 30). This capacity comes from Yahweh (2:7), and it provides ability in practical affairs, such as in governmental rule (8:14, *cf.* 8:15–16).[3] Sound judgment leads to success in the practical matters of life, which provides one with confidence and safety (3:21, *cf.* 3:22–26).

The term 'wise dealing' (*śēkel*), used once in a verbal construction (1:3) and once as a noun (3:4), speaks of good sense of what is right, just and fair, as the parallelism in 1:3 suggests. As Aitken (1986: 11–12) observes:

> In the Old Testament these are the great qualities of conduct which make for the good and well-being of

---

[3] Whybray (1994b: 125) notes the similar language and emphases in Pr. 8:14–16; Is. 11:2; and Jb. 12:13: 'This employment of identical or equivalent terms in all three passages can hardly be entirely coincidental. It appears from the passages in Job and Isaiah that these were terms applied in the wisdom tradition to God, but also, in a secondary sense, to kings who ruled in his name. In Prov. 8:14–15, however, it is Wisdom who claims, in similar terms, to be the source of all political authority and power.'

the community: one in which all men play by the rules, where one man's rights are as important as another's, and where honesty and integrity are the only policies.

It is insightfulness which leads to success, as the verbal form especially indicates as it describes the intelligent actions of Abigail, who brought a potentially disastrous situation to a successful conclusion (1 Sa. 25:3ff.).

A key set of terms speaking of 'competence in understanding' is drawn from the root *byn*. The verb *bîn* is found eight times, and the synonyms *bînâ* and *tᵉbûnâ*[4] combined are used eighteen times. The root sense of this lexical family is seen in the related preposition *bayin*, 'between'. Consequently, the verb means 'to discern between competing alternatives'. Solomon prays for this ability in 1 Kings 3:9, when he says, 'So give your servant a discerning heart to govern your people and to distinguish [*hābîn*] between right and wrong.' More than mere acquisition of knowledge, it is the capacity 'to compare concepts and form judgments or establish analogies' (Greenstone 1950: 3, citing *Pirke Aboth* III:21). It describes the exercise of moral insight, by which that which is right, just and fair is understood (Pr. 2:9).[5] To understand is to make good choices between alternative possibilities. The standard for evaluating these decisions is the fear of Yahweh (2:5), for independent judgments must be made within the bounds of his moral order (McKane 1970: 266).

The uses of the nouns *bînâ* and *tᵉbûnâ* agree with the range of meaning indicated by the verb. Understanding has a strong theological orientation, for it was the basis of Yahweh's creative activity (Pr. 3:19), and it is rooted in the knowledge of the Holy One (9:10). Through understanding one can exercise ethical discernment (7:4–5), perceptive insight (9:6), and the ability to rule (8:14–16). One must not, however, lean on one's own

---

[4] In Pr. 2:3, the two nouns are used in synonymous parallelism: '. . . and if you call for insight [*bînâ*] and cry aloud for understanding [*tᵉbûnâ*].'

[5] McKane (1970: 283) expounds the significance of *bîn* in the context of Pr. 2: 'The metaphor which is sustained in this passage is that of the two ways (vv. 7, 8, 9, 12, 13, 15, 18, 19, 20), and in view of this we may say that righteousness is the state of the man who walks in Yahweh's ways. He who discerns Yahweh's order for his community and who brings his way of life – the web of his relationships – into harmony with it is *ṣaddîq*. These are plain, level roads along which good progress can be made.'

understanding apart from trust in Yahweh (3:5),[6] for as Green-stone (1950: 27) remarks,

> Human understanding is not always reliable and has to look for support to divine guidance. Understanding is important and one should make every effort to attain it, but one should not rely on it entirely, since experience has shown that it is fallible and has to have divine support.

The final term reflecting competence is 'wisdom'. The verb *ḥākam*, the adjective *ḥākām*, and the noun *ḥokmâ* are used a total of twenty-six times in Proverbs 1 – 9. Wisdom is not a native ability for humans, but it must be chosen consciously (9:12). Thus, each person can choose the path of wisdom with its attendant rewards or the path of folly with its inevitable penalties.

Just as one must not lean on one's own understanding (3:5), so the teacher warns against self-reliant wisdom: 'Do not be wise in your own eyes; fear the LORD and shun evil' (3:7). Zornberg (1982: 32) elaborates on this important caution:

> Since the moral law is not something that can be known empirically, there are men who conclude that whatever way they choose is *ipso facto* moral. This is an individualistic, relativistic morality, that acknowledges no superior absolute authority. True morality, however, says the master of proverbs, comes only from the Almighty, and is often uncongenial to man's wishes; and it can therefore be accepted only if there is a prior experience of 'fear of God' which can lead a man to abdicate his own autonomy in defining his moral code.

---

[6] Whybray (1994b: 63) is right when he rejects the claim by McKane (1970: 292) that understanding in Pr. 3:5 'is a sinful hubris which is incompatible with trust in Yahweh'. As the uses of *bînâ* in Is. 29:14, 24, indicate, the term can be used of genuine understanding based in trust in Yahweh or of a supposed insight which people illegitimately claim for themselves. It is not, as McKane alleges, that the term has been transmuted from an original intellectual notion into a religious concept, but that the semantic range of *bînâ* encompassed both legitimate and illegitimate senses of understanding. In a similar way, trust (*bāṭaḥ*) can be used of both confidence in Yahweh (Pr. 3:5) and of a false sense of security (Jdg. 18:7, 10, 27).

The biblical concept of wisdom is not speculative, but it is intensely practical. Across the broad range of life, including such diverse activities as artistic craftsmanship (Ex. 31:36), marine navigation (Ps. 107:27), government administration (1 Ki. 3:28) and personal counsel (2 Sa. 20:22), *ḥokmâ* speaks of 'skillfulness in dealing with the matter at hand so as to get the best results' (Aitken 1986: 10; *cf.* Ross 1991: 904–905).[7] The wise person is 'above all the man who could teach others because he had superior understanding about how life should be lived and what it means' (Scott 1971: 3).

True wisdom finds its ultimate source in Yahweh, for 'the LORD gives wisdom, and from his mouth come knowledge and understanding' (Pr. 2:6).[8] It was by wisdom that Yahweh laid the earth's foundations (3:19, expanded in 8:22–31). The fear of Yahweh is the beginning of wisdom (9:10), for wisdom has no independent status apart from him. True wisdom and true faith are correlatives, not antitheses, for 'without this basic reverence for Yahweh and submission to him, there can be no acquisition of wisdom . . .' (McKane 1970: 264). Those who refuse to reverence Yahweh are fools who despise wisdom (1:7).

Wisdom is a blessing which must be found (3:13). Some aspects of it can be discovered from observation of the natural world, for the teacher exhorts the sluggard, 'Go to the ant . . . consider its ways and be wise!' (6:6). More frequently, however, wisdom is learned by heeding instruction (1:5; 2:2; 5:1; 8:33;

[7] Fox (1968: 55) gives a more comprehensive description of the semantic range of the term: 'The word *ḥokmā* includes four distinct senses: (1) practical sagacity – the knowledge and ability that cause a man to succeed in his everyday life and occupation (three subcategories of this sense are: (a) general reasoning ability, ability to comprehend, native intelligence; (b) statecraft – the ability and knowledge necessary for a ruler and his advisors; (c) technical knowledge – craftsmanship, skill); (2) ethical-religious wisdom – the type of wisdom recommended and exemplified by the Book of Proverbs; (3) speculative wisdom – understanding of life and the phenomenal world; (4) an intellectual technique for attaining this speculative wisdom, a discipline of learning (as opposed to the knowledge itself that comes from this intellectual discipline). The latter is Qoheleth's usage.'

[8] Whybray (1994b: 52) notes: '. . . the placing of *the Lord* at the beginning of the sentence in the Hebrew instead of in its normal position following the verb gives it a strong emphasis. The pupil is now told that only God can give what the pupil is told to seek to attain in attending to the teacher and in searching for Wisdom.'

9:9). This need for a receptive attitude parallels the similar emphasis in the Egyptian Instruction texts:

> ... the demand for receptivity is prominent in the Egyptian Instruction, and it is a willingness to assimilate a body of traditional wisdom rather than any show of originality which is expected of the apprentice sage. This does not mean that the educational process is no more than the mechanical memorizing of information. Rather, it is the belief that no man can be wise who has not steeped himself in that wisdom which is the deposit of the best minds of many generations (McKane 1970: 266).

This receptivity is expressed in accepting both positive instruction and negative criticism (9:8b).

When wisdom is received, it enters the heart (2:10), so that it can function as the dominant factor controlling the person's thoughts, emotions and decisions. As the parallel line indicates, when wisdom enters the heart, then knowledge becomes pleasant to the soul. Ross notes, 'When a person assimilates wisdom, doing right becomes attractive and delightful; for he sees the advantage of it' (1991: 913).

Wisdom also equips its possessor to handle proverbial sayings with their reflections on life. One of the stated goals of the book of Proverbs is to prepare the learner 'for understanding proverbs and parables, the sayings and riddles of the wise' (1:6). By employing a variety of rhetorical devices the teacher seeks to involve the learner in grappling with the mysterious and enigmatic features of life. Skill in living requires both understanding of observable phenomena and sensitivity to the more ambiguous elements of life.

Ultimately, wisdom has a practical orientation, for it is skill in living in Yahweh's world as he intends life to be lived. Reverencing Yahweh as the source of wisdom, listening to the accumulated insights of the past, observing life as it functions in the present, and probing the enigmas which yet await full understanding, the wise person develops competence in living as Yahweh desires. This skill enables him to become a teacher of others who seek wisdom.

These seven terms, then, all speak of the competence which

wisdom seeks to develop in the learner. The goal of education is more than the transmission of knowledge from the teacher to the student. Rather, education strives to develop in the learner independent competence, the skill necessary to function well in Yahweh's world.

Protection

Proverbs 1 – 9 is intensely realistic, for it recognizes throughout that evil exists in the world. Instead of painting an idealistic world without ethical tension, wisdom describes the harmful influences that imperil the learner, and it teaches how these dangerous threats can be avoided. Commenting on Proverbs 2, Newsom (1989: 146–147) explains the strategy employed by wisdom:

> The world is presented as a place of competing and conflicting discourses: the words of the father, the words of the crooked man, the words of the strange woman. One is hailed from many directions, offered subject positions in discourses that construe the world very differently. Far from valuing the plurality of discourses that intersect a culture, Proverbs 1 – 9 seeks the hegemony of its own discourse. If one has internalized a discourse, one is insulated from, or as the text more polemically puts it, protected from other voices.

In this section, the learner is counselled against four categories of evil which can entice him away from Yahweh's way: personal vices, peers, evil men and evil women.

As discussed in the previous chapter, Proverbs 1:22 mentions three types of people who resist the teaching of wisdom (see pages 46–47). Each of these traits reflects a personal vice from which the learner needs protection. The vice of simplicity (*petî*) speaks of gullibility. The simple person is tossed about by whatever seems appealing at the moment, because he does not have a moral compass to give him reliable bearings. Consequently, the simple person develops a wayward approach to life (1:32), smugly satisfied that he knows better how to live (Aitken 1986: 25). This can lead to impulsive commitments, perhaps given out of honourable motives, but none the less placing the simple person at great risk. In the example in Proverbs 6:1–5, the teacher states that if a man has put up security for the loan of another, he should by all means extricate himself from this trap, even if it means humbling himself before the creditor. Furthermore, simplicity can lead to sluggishness, a lack of alertness and foresight which undermines effective work (6:9–11). As McKane (1970: 324) describes the sluggard:

> . . . he is so sleepy-headed he has no defences against the onset of poverty and privation; he eats and sleeps from day to day, and when he is not unconscious he lives in a no-man's land between sleep and waking life, his intelligence drugged by somnolence.

The mocker (*lēṣ*), or scoffer, embodies the vice of arrogant rejection of the counsel of others. Instead of welcoming instruction, a mocking attitude insults and hates the one who gives the rebuke (Pr. 9:7–8; *cf.* 1:25, 30). Nurtured by pride (note the contrast with the humble in 3:34), the mocker supposes himself to be beyond the need for direction and correction. This haughty rejection of what wisdom seeks to teach, however, leads to personal disaster (9:12b).

Folly (*keSîl*) refers to self-satisfied stupidity. The foolish person is morally insensitive and does not listen to reason (Ross 1991: 910). He is wilfully indifferent, because he hates knowledge and refuses to choose the fear of Yahweh as the principle for his life (1:29). As Proverbs 1:32 teaches, the complacency of fools makes them unwilling to learn, for they are controlled by 'the vast and imperturbable self-satisfaction of the man who has nothing to learn from anyone and who is impervious to instruction' (McKane 1970: 276). Although Proverbs 5:23 uses a different word for folly (*'iwwelet*), its collocation of folly with the lack of discipline (*mûsār*) is instructive. The term *mûsār* is a key concept in Proverbs 1 – 9, referring to life under control. It speaks of 'discipline exercised by one in command – whether God, a father or human teacher, or "Wisdom" – over those in his charge' (Whybray 1994b: 32). Fools despise wisdom and discipline because they do not reverence Yahweh (1:7; *cf.* 3:11). In addition, they fail to listen to human teachers (1:8; 4:1; 5:12–13; 6:23). Because *mûsār* emanates from wisdom (8:10, 33), those characterized by folly do not possess the skill for living which wisdom provides.

In addition to protecting the learner from the personal vices engendered by simplicity, mocking and folly, wisdom also warns him against pressures from peers. The exhortation that follows the prologue to Proverbs 1 – 9 is grounded in real life as it describes the power of temptation and defends against its threat. The sinners seeking to entice the learner urge him to follow them on a quick route to excitement, money and acceptance. As Aitken (1986: 19) observes, this temptation is particularly alluring, because it activates his legitimate desires for adventure, independence and friendship. They invite him to join them in a spree of gratuitous violence (1:11–12), which will lead to easy money (1:13). He would be a full partner of the gang, sharing equally in the common purse (1:14). The teacher warns him, however, against the peers, because their path will lead to evil, entrapment and death (1:15–19). Their sinful attitude blinds them to inevitable judgment which will befall them, for they are like birds who see a net spread, and yet they fly into it.

A third danger from which the learner needs protection is evil men (*cf.* pages 49–50). As described in Proverbs 2:12–15, the evil men are perverse, or twisted, because they have abandoned Yahweh's straight paths in order to walk in dark ways. They invert Yahweh's values, delighting in doing wrong and rejoicing in evil. Wisdom is designed to save the learner from the ways of evil men (2:12a), protecting him from the ethical chaos which they promote (McKane 1970: 284). In Proverbs 4:14–19 the teacher warns the student to avoid the way of evil men, because they live only to do what is wrong. Unlike the path of the righteous which leads to increased moral illumination, the way of the wicked is like the deep darkness[9] of ignorance and insecurity.

---

[9] Aitken (1986: 58) discusses the Hebrew term *'ªpēlâ*, translated 'deep darkness' in Pr. 4:19: 'There is always something uncanny about this darkness. It is the darkness which enveloped the land of Egypt as one of the plagues (Exod. 10:22); while the prophets speak of it in their descriptions of that terrifying day of divine judgment, the "Day of the Lord" (Joel 2:2; Amos 5:20; Zeph. 1:15). The word suggests the dreadful extent of their moral blindness, having spurned wisdom's light (1:23–25, 29–30). But more especially, it points to what is bound to happen to those who walk along a twisting road in total darkness.'

The fourth, and predominant, harmful influence that threatens the learner is the evil, or strange, woman (see earlier discussion on pages 54–57).[10] Throughout Proverbs 1 – 9 this evil woman representing folly is the rival of wisdom, who appeals to the young man to embrace her. The invitation by folly in Proverbs 9:13–18 is a clear parody of the call of wisdom in Proverbs 9:1–6. Unlike wisdom, who challenges her hearers to follow her to life and understanding, however, folly appeals to the baser instincts (9:17). The references to stolen water and food eaten in secret allude to illicit sexual activity (*cf.* 5:15–18; 7:14).[11] Nevertheless, the tempting offer by folly leads inevitably to death (9:18), in all of its dimensions.[12]

Wisdom, then, has as a defensive goal the protection of the learner from the harmful influences that could easily lead to disaster. By describing the threats of personal vices, peers, the evil man and the evil woman, wisdom enables the novice to be forewarned of the dangers which lurk in the real world. By defining their deleterious effects, wisdom motivates the learner to avoid the temptation to choose immediate pleasures over what is of eternal value. By exhorting the youth to stand firm against invitations to sin, wisdom seeks to protect him from folly by keeping him firmly committed to the way of Yahweh.

[10] The subject of the evil or strange woman has spawned a vast amount of research. In addition to discussions in the standard commentaries, the following recent specialized studies are useful: Blenkinsopp (1991); Camp (1985 and 1991); Hadley (1995); Kruger (1987); Newsom (1989); O'Connell (1991); and Yee (1989).

[11] Whybray (1994b: 148–149) develops this point well: 'This verse corresponds with v. 5 in that "food" and "drink" are offered as inducements; but the point is the complete contrast between the true nature of what is offered in the respective cases. Wisdom offers instruction for the mind; Folly offers sexual pleasure. *water* (not the "wine" offered by Wisdom) is a metaphor for sexual intercourse as in 5:15; its being *stolen* means that it is forbidden and clandestine. *bread eaten in secret*: eating is a frequent metaphor for sexual intercourse: compare 30:20. *sweet, pleasant*: the clandestine nature of the action proposed makes it all the more desirable.'

[12] Murphy (1981b: 26) expounds the semantic range of death in the wisdom literature: 'Opposed to life is death, which is an equally elastic concept. It is more than drawing one's final breath before departing for Sheol. It is all the non-life that humans experience: adversity, suffering, disaster. The synonym for death is Sheol, or the nether world. One is never more dead than when one is in Sheol, the deepest point of death.'

Prosperity

Although the biblical wisdom literature corpus as a whole recognizes that life is at times mysterious and unpredictable because the ways of Yahweh are inscrutable to humans, Proverbs 1 – 9 focuses upon the general correlation between acts and consequences in Yahweh's ordered world. In keeping with this commitment to retribution theology, one of the chief goals of education in this section is that the learner may become prosperous across the broad range of life. The way of wisdom is recommended, because it will lead to prosperity in his personal life, his social relationships, and his relationship with Yahweh.

Whereas the path of folly leads to death (1:19; 2:18; 5:5; 7:23; 9:18), wisdom leads to life. Personified wisdom states in Proverbs 8:35a, 36: 'For whoever finds me finds life . . . but whoever fails to find me harms himself; all who hate me love death.' Though education is indeed designed to cultivate the skills necessary for a successful career, it has the even greater purpose of nurturing a good and successful life (Aitken 1986: 3–4).

'Life' in Proverbs 1 – 9 is a comprehensive term for well-being. As Perdue (1994: 92) observes,

> Life refers to a wide range of values and desired experiences, from longevity to prosperity to good health to family to love to outer and inner harmony and to 'success' in one's deeds. The state of well-being is another way of expressing wisdom's view of life.

This sense of life is summed up by the term šālôm, which speaks of completeness and wholeness, 'all the factors which make existence complete and worthwhile' (Cohen 1952: 13).

Proverbs focuses on life in the present, in keeping with the predominant Old Testament emphasis on temporal life as the context for living for Yahweh (cf. Pss. 6:5[6]; 26:9[10]; 88:11[12]). Beyond life on earth only the shadowy world of Sheol greets humans (McKane 1970: 22), so life must be enjoyed in the present if it is to be enjoyed at all. Life is typically viewed in qualitative terms, but the quantitative notion of long life also is important. The teacher, therefore, exhorts the youth, 'Listen, my son, accept what I say, and the years of your life will be many'

(Pr. 4:10), and wisdom itself promises, 'For through me your days will be many, and years will be added to your life' (9:11).

A constituent element of life is success. The one who listens to wisdom will 'be at ease, without fear of harm' (1:33b). The term translated 'harm' is *rāʿâ*, which speaks of misfortune or calamity. Instead of this disaster, the one who lives wisely by acknowledging Yahweh in all of his ways will find that Yahweh will make his paths straight (3:6) by removing obstacles from them (*cf.* Is. 40:3; 45:2; Pr. 11:5). A goal of wisdom, then, is to enable the learner to make his way successfully in the world (McKane 1970: 265), smoothing his way so that he need not fear misfortune.

The life which wisdom provides is also characterized by stability. The teacher develops this point by means of contrast in Proverbs 2:21–22:

> For the upright will live in the land,
>   and the blameless will remain in it;
> but the wicked will be cut off from the land,
>   and the unfaithful will be torn from it.

'The land' here refers most likely to the land of Canaan, promised by covenant to Israel. Continuance in the land was conditioned by obedience to the law of Yahweh, so following the dictates of wisdom that are rooted in the fear of Yahweh would guarantee continued stability in the land. The same truth is taught by means of a different metaphor in Proverbs 4:18–19, in which the path of the righteous is like ever-increasing light which facilitates stable walking, but the way of the wicked is like deep darkness which causes them to stumble because they cannot see their path.[13]

Wisdom also holds out the prospect of material wealth to those who follow her. In contrast with the pursuit of ill-gotten

---

[13] Aitken (1986: 57) remarks well: 'The picture is one of the steady increase in the brightness and intensity of the daylight, from the first flickers of dawn to the brilliant radiance of the noonday sun which bathes the whole landscape in its light. With the light of wisdom to guide him (6:23; *cf.* Ps. 119:105) and to light up the road ahead, the pilgrim can see where he is going, and knows where, and where not, to place his feet. No loose stones, pot-holes or icy patches find shadows to lurk behind to catch him unawares. The way of wisdom is therefore the safe and secure road through life, and it leads to fullness of life (v. 10; 6:23).'

gain which impoverishes and destroys humans (Pr. 1:19), those who honour Yahweh with the firstfruits of their income will be rewarded with overflowing abundance (3:9–10). Not only does wisdom possess and dispense long life, but she also is the repository of riches and honour (3:16).[14] The fact that wisdom holds long life in her right hand, and riches and honour in her left, may well indicate the relative worth of the blessings. According to Genesis 48:14 the right hand was the hand of chief blessing, and the left hand indicated lesser status. Thus, the teacher may be suggesting that 'even at its most materialistic, wisdom offers a man no encouragement to give his life to making money' (Aitken 1986: 47).

In addition, the life which wisdom gives enjoys health and vitality. As Proverbs 3:7–8 teaches, fearing Yahweh and shunning evil brings health to the body and nourishment to the bones. The learner is enjoined to keep the teacher's words within his heart, 'for they are life to those who find them and health to a man's whole body' (4:22).

A further incentive for adopting the way of wisdom is the honour that it gives. From Yahweh the wise inherit honour, but he holds up the fools to shame (3:35). As Barucq (1964: 65) remarks, this honour is not eschatological glory in heaven, as is taught in the New Testament (2 Cor. 4:17–18), but it refers to honour and reputation on earth. The parallel words in Proverbs 4:8–9 indicate that those who honour wisdom will in turn be honoured by her:

> Esteem her, and she will exalt you;
>   embrace her, and she will honour you.
> She will set a garland of grace on your head
>   and present you with a crown of splendour.

As in Proverbs 12:4; 14:24; 16:31 and 17:6, the metaphor of the crown speaks of stature within the community, for wisdom produces favour and a good name with humans, as well as with God (3:4).

The culmination of the blessing of life is the satisfaction and happiness that the wise person enjoys. This satisfaction is found

---

[14] In a similar fashion, the Egyptian goddess *Maat* is pictured as holding symbols of life, riches and honour in her hands (Kayatz 1966: 105–106).

in part in the delights of marriage as the young man rejoices in the wife of his youth (5:18–19). More generally, wisdom is a tree of life to those who embrace her (3:18). This image (see pages 58–59) speaks of the continual source of happiness that wisdom provides to those who follow her way.

Although the predominant context of prosperity in Proverbs 1 – 9 is the personal life of the learner, there are also wider dimensions discussed. Not only does wisdom bless the individual, but it also enriches the society. Contrary to foolish actions, which are socially destructive (cf. 6:12–19, 29–35) because they 'break the bond of confidence and loyalty between man and man' (McKane 1970: 326), wisdom brings harmony to society. Hoppe (1981: 156) remarks:

> What was the purpose of all this advice that the sages were so willing to give to so many different people? One basic concern of the sages was to promote the harmony and well-being of ancient Israelite society. They wished to help people order their lives in such a way that a positive social climate could be created. The sages wanted to enable the community to function optimally. They recognized the necessity of experience, respect for parents and elders, the welfare of children, good government, respect for property and protection of the poor. Otherwise, the community faced self-destruction.

The instructions in Proverbs 3:27–30 illustrate how wisdom contributes to social cohesion. The teacher challenges the learner to do good to his neighbour when he has the resources to do so, rather than putting him off with excuses. Moreover, he must not plot harm against his neighbour, or accuse him for no reason. Wisdom, then, strikes at the heart of both selfish independence and malicious competitiveness. Instead of these deficient values, wisdom promotes a commitment to neighbourliness, 'creating an environment where social stability could produce its natural fruits' (Cox 1987: 10; cf. Clements 1993: 228).

In its ultimate form, prosperity is viewed as the enjoyment of Yahweh's favour. Wisdom proclaims, 'For whoever finds me finds life and receives favour from the LORD' (Pr. 8:35; cf. 3:4).

Supporting this explicit statement is the implicit witness of Proverbs 2:21. Since continued life in the land is predicated on the blessing of Yahweh in accordance with his covenant prescriptions, the fact that the upright will live in the land indicates that they enjoy his favour.

In Proverbs 1 – 9 education seeks to produce prosperity for the learner. Following the way of wisdom leads to personal life in its multiple facets of success, stability, wealth, health, honour and satisfaction. In the broader perspective, wisdom builds the kind of social relationships that contribute to stability and harmony in the community. Best of all, the person who learns wisdom enjoys the favour of Yahweh and the blessings which that entails.

Knowledge of God

Towering above all of the other goals of education in Proverbs 1 – 9 is the ultimate prize of the knowledge of God. The fear of Yahweh is the beginning of wisdom (Pr. 9:10), and it is also the consummate end of wisdom (2:5). Education, then, should produce in the learner more than just a sense of achievement; it should also cultivate reverence for Yahweh and an intimate personal fellowship with him (Toombs 1955: 194–195).

As Zornberg (1982: 23) states well, the relationship between reverence and wisdom, or between fear and understanding, is dynamic, working in both directions. On the one hand, the fear of Yahweh is the fundamental value that grounds education. On the other hand, the search for wisdom leads eventually to the knowledge of God. Zornberg says:

> . . . fear induces knowledge, the lucid acceptance of the moral law and its dictates; but man can then press onwards from this quiescent base to a resumed pursuit of the more esoteric 'knowledge of God', of the mysteries of His being and His relation to the world; this, in turn, naturally brings in its train a new intensity of awe through the newly comprehended sublimity.

Proverbs 9:10 states, 'The fear of the LORD is the beginning of wisdom, and knowledge of the Holy One is understanding.' Though the learner must submit to the tutelage of the human teacher of wisdom, the ultimate goal is that he might reverence Yahweh. Though it is vital that the student learn to navigate successfully through life in human society, it is even more crucial that he learn to know God through a vibrant faith and commitment to him (McKane 1970: 368). While actively engaged in the full range of affairs in human life, the learner must seek to know Yahweh by reverencing him through submission to his standards. Knowledge of God, then, is not divorced from everyday life, as though belonging to a sacred sphere separate from the secular life. Instead, the knowledge of God is the pre-eminent goal that is the integration point for all of life.

In this emphasis Proverbs 1 – 9 agrees with the prophetic emphasis on the knowledge of God (Farmer 1991: 31). For example, Hosea 4:1 defines Yahweh's legal dispute with Israel in these terms: 'There is no faithfulness, no love, no acknowledgment [*da'at* = knowledge] of God in the land.' Isaiah 1:3 records the words of Yahweh to the sinful nation: 'The ox knows his master, the donkey his owner's manger, but Israel does not know, my people do not understand.' Ezekiel's frequent refrain is that 'then they will know that I am the LORD'. The overarching goal for humans, then, in both the wisdom tradition and in the prophetic tradition is 'an ethical reaction to the will of God, an emotional recognition of the manifestations of God in nature and in history, as the force for truth, justice and kindness' (Greenstone 1950: 18).

Conclusion

The goals for education stated in Proverbs 1 – 9 focus for the most part on the cultivation of the learner as a mature godly person, rather than upon the transmission of a discrete body of knowledge. The teacher endeavours to create in the learner a personal commitment to diligence, discipline and devotion to wisdom. In other words, a primary goal for education is that the learner may accept for himself the values that wisdom propounds so that his life is shaped according to Yahweh's desires.

Closely related to the goal of commitment is the emphasis on the development of godly character. This quality of character provides the learner with an internal compulsion to keep learning and growing in wisdom.

The emphasis in Proverbs 1 – 9 on the development of the learner's competence, or skill in living, is communicated through seven key Hebrew terms: *'ormâ* (prudence), *mᵉzimmâ* (discretion), *taḥbulâ* (guidance), *tûšîyyâ* (sound judgment), *śēkel* (wise dealing), *byn* (understanding) and *ḥkm* (wisdom). The aggregate sense of these terms is that education endeavours to develop in the learner the competence necessary to function independently as a godly person in Yahweh's world.

Proverbs 1 – 9 also seeks to protect the learner from the dangerous influences that can harm his life. By portraying realistic pictures of enticements to sin, the teacher forewarns the learner against the threats from personal vices, peers, evil men and evil women. Thus, wisdom has both developmental and preventative goals.

As an incentive for the learner to accept the way of wisdom, the teacher describes the prosperity that wisdom affords. In the area of personal life, Yahweh's way of wisdom leads to well-being, success, stability, wealth, health, honour and satisfaction. Wisdom also enriches social relationships by providing intrinsic cohesion to counteract the impulses of human independence and competitiveness. Furthermore, education in wisdom enables the learner to enjoy the blessings that Yahweh bestows on those whom he favours.

The ultimate goal for education in Proverbs 1 – 9 is the knowledge of God. Just as the fear of Yahweh is the beginning of wisdom (9:10), so it is the end of wisdom as well (2:5). The knowledge of God is the supreme goal that draws all of education and life together into an integrated whole.

Chapter Four

Curriculum for education

As discussed in chapter 3, the goals for education developed in Proverbs 1 – 9 focus on the moral and ethical development of the learner, culminating in the knowledge of God. Craigie (1979: 8) rightly concludes:

> . . . the role of education was not merely to instruct the young concerning how to make a living but also to direct them concerning how to live. No amount of professional skill would lead to a successful and valuable life, unless it was accompanied by moral wisdom.

Although the pursuit of knowledge for its own sake is not a prominent goal in biblical wisdom in general, or in Proverbs 1 – 9 in particular, knowledge is an important means to the desired end of the learner's growth. The teacher employs a body of information in instructing the student. This subject matter, or curriculum, for education is the concern of the present chapter.

The wisdom literature uses a wide variety of materials drawn from numerous settings in life as it seeks to instruct the learner.[1] The full range of experience in God's world is mined, from

---

[1] Crenshaw (1969: 130) defines several types of wisdom literature and speculates on their probable settings and methods: 'It must be recognized that wisdom speech is not *a se* wisdom, and that several kinds of wisdom are discernible: (1) juridical, (2) nature, (3) practical, and (4) theological – each with a distinct *Sitz im Leben*. Accordingly, one must distinguish between family/ clan wisdom, the goal of which is the mastering of life, the stance hortatory and style proverbial; court wisdom, with the goal of education for a select group, the stance secular, and the method didactic; and scribal wisdom, the goal being education for all, the stance dogmatico-religious, and the method dialogico-admonitory.' His classifications may well be overly precise, because similar forms can be used in different settings for diverse purposes, but his general point about the variety within wisdom literature is sound.

observations of the smallest animals (Pr. 6:6–8; 30:24–28) to the profound questions of evil (Job) and human significance (Ecclesiastes). At the root of wisdom's concern is the search for meaning within Yahweh's world. Crenshaw (1969: 132) observes that this search moves on three levels: nature wisdom observes and draws lessons from features in the physical world, practical wisdom focuses on human relationships within a social order, and theological wisdom affirms God as the repository of ultimate meaning despite the nettlesome problems which life presents. Although Proverbs 1 – 9 is but a small segment of the biblical wisdom corpus, each of these three types of wisdom can be found within it.

The wisdom literature, including Proverbs 1 – 9, nearly always views life in generic terms. Unlike the legal, historical, prophetic and hymnic literature of the Old Testament, the wisdom texts contain no explicit references to events in the history of Israel. In addition, few allusions to distinctive cultic obligations can be identified. This absence of data unique to Israel is not likely to be accidental, but it is probably 'due to the specific intention of wisdom writers to express truths and deal with problems that are timeless and common to all peoples' (Boström 1990: 33).

The subject matter constituting the curriculum for education in Proverbs 1 – 9 can be organized into three categories. First, observations of the world examine the physical environment and human behaviour to draw lessons about the order which Yahweh has embedded in them. Second, tradition both from within Israel and from other ancient Near Eastern cultures is presented as a reliable source of knowledge. Third, by revelation humans learn from Yahweh information that would not otherwise be discernible by them.

Observation

On occasion the wisdom teacher challenges the learner to make personal, immediate insights by observing the physical world of nature and human behaviour in society. Only rarely is personal observation used as a source of knowledge in Proverbs 1 – 9, the teacher preferring to employ a more direct approach of instruction.

Beginning with the premise that the world as created by Yahweh demonstrates order, the pedagogy of wisdom observes the physical world and then draws inferences for human behaviour from what it sees.[2] Just as nature psalms such as Psalms 19 and 104 affirm that the physical world pours forth information about God, so the wisdom literature looks to nature to understand divine truth. For example, Job challenges his friends to learn from the creation that Yahweh sovereignly upholds the world he has made:

> But ask the animals, and they will teach you,
>   or the birds of the air, and they will tell you;
> or speak to the earth, and it will teach you,
>   or let the fish of the sea inform you.
> Which of all these does not know
>   that the hand of the LORD has done this?
> In his hand is the life of every creature
>   and the breath of all mankind (Jb. 12:7–10).

In his majestic response to Job in Job 38:2 – 41:34, Yahweh points him to the physical world, posing probing questions to guide Job into insight and submission.

The single passage in Proverbs 1 – 9 that uses personal observation of the physical world is Proverbs 6:6–8, although even this example suggests a degree of involvement by the teacher:

> Go to the ant, you sluggard;
>   consider its ways and be wise!
> It has no commander,
>   no overseer or ruler,
> yet it stores its provisions in summer
>   and gathers its food at harvest.

It is evident that the ant is not used as a fable, but the learner is counselled to make literal observations of the actions of the

---

[2] Crenshaw (1981a: 209) notes: 'Nothing within human experience lacked revelatory capacity. No vision of past glory or future hope robbed the present moment of its importance. For this reason every encounter afforded a bridge into the transcendent realm. The slightest act by an insect, or the behavior of humans, concealed a secret worthy of discovery. In this way all of life became an arena in which divine truth unfolded, and God's truth coincided with human insight.'

animal. McKane (1970: 323–324) distinguishes between these two different approaches:

> In the fable, human behaviour is attributed to plants and animals and a situation is contrived which throws some light on human behaviour and relationships, or which constitutes a comment, perhaps satirical, on human institutions. The use of the ant as a paradigm in this passage is less artful and more heavily didactic than fable, and there is no metamorphosis of the insect. What is in view is the ant *qua* ant, whose habits are analogous to those of the disciplined, methodical and diligent man.

By going to the ant, observing it, and considering the implications of what it does, the learner can gain wisdom.

In Proverbs 6:7–8 the teacher suggests some of the perceptive insights which can be drawn by careful personal observation of the ant. The ant takes initiative and works industriously without external compulsion. Without extrinsic motivation from commander, overseer or ruler, the ant does what is necessary to provide for its anticipated needs, a point also observed in Proverbs 30:25. Thus, 'the ant is described as acting autonomously, without the kinds of motivation, direction and regulation that operate in human society' (Zornberg 1982: 60).

In addition to observing the physical world, wisdom also observes and learns from the full range of human activities. Assuming that human nature is more or less a constant (Cox 1982b: 5–6), wisdom uses what it sees in the lives of people to develop lessons for constructive behaviour.

The only example in Proverbs 1 – 9 in which the learner is urged to make personal observations from human life is found in Proverbs 5:15–20. In this passage the son is challenged to find satisfaction from sexual intimacy with his wife, clearly to fortify him against the enticements of the evil, or strange, woman. The teacher says:

> Drink water from your own cistern,
>   running water from your own well.
> Should your springs overflow in the streets,

your streams of water in the public squares?[3]
Let them be yours alone,
   never to be shared with strangers.
May your fountain be blessed,
   and may you rejoice in the wife of your youth.
A loving doe, a graceful deer –
   may her breasts satisfy you always,
   may you ever be captivated[4] by her love.
Why be captivated, my son, by an adulteress?
Why embrace the bosom of another man's wife?[5]

---

[3] Translations and commentators are divided as to whether verse 16 should be construed as a statement (AV) or as a question (most modern translations). As a statement the verse makes a positive affirmation, 'Your springs will overflow in the streets, your streams of water in the public squares,' that speaks of the unending abundance of satisfaction which can be derived from proper sexual intimacy in marriage. As a question the verse gives a negative admonition against promiscuity that squanders the satisfaction which could be gained through legitimate means. There is nothing in the Hebrew text, such as an interrogative particle, to suggest that the verse should be construed as a question, although an interrogative marker is not absolutely necessary. On the other hand, reading verse 16 as a question suits the exclusive language of verses 15 and 17, especially if streams of water in the public squares represents treating what should be priceless and exclusive as cheap and common. *Cf.* Kidner (1964: 70); Whybray (1994b: 89–90).

[4] Garrett (1993: 94) points out the significance of the catchword *šāgâ* found in verses 19 ('captivated'), 20 ('captivated'), and 23 ('led astray'): 'A man will stagger in the pleasure his wife gives (v. 19). He can embrace the bosom of another woman and stagger (v. 20), but the terms of sensual pleasure are absent here; with the adulteress it is the staggering of confusion and weakness. Finally, the man who indulges in adultery will stagger to his own destruction (v. 23).'

[5] Kruger (1987: 66–67) gives an insightful analysis of this text: 'Scholars have failed to detect that the whole allegory rests on the matter of *private* versus *common* property; the *own cistern* (v 15) as against the springs and channels of water in the street (v 16); the water which belongs to you *alone* (v 17) in opposition to those in the open places which is the property of *foreigners* (*zārîm*, v 17). The cistern which usually was *privately* owned in the Old Testament times (II Kings 18:13 = Is 36:16) gives point to this metaphor.

'Over and against this privately owned possession (v 15) appears "the rivulets of water in the open places" (v 16), symbol of common property to which each and everyone has access. If we remain in the spirit of the woman imagery of the first part of Proverbs (1 – 9) it is not difficult to discover that these water-sources on the street and in open places are metaphorical depictions of the figure of the unchaste woman (*'iššâ zārā/nokrîyyâ*) and her characteristic kind of conduct.'

As in Proverbs 6:6–8, so in Proverbs 5:15–20 the teacher goes beyond directing the learner to personal observation to state the insights that he should discover as he enjoys intimacy with his wife. Nevertheless, it is the learner who is personally involved in observing that satisfaction is best found within the legitimate bounds of marriage, not through illicit sexual activity.[6]

Tradition

In addition to personal, immediate observation of life, wisdom also draws upon the legacy of past tradition for its body of knowledge. Through attention to what others have observed, the student is able to augment what he himself has discovered through experience. The book of Proverbs represents traditional knowledge, for it contains 'the accumulated wisdom of past generations distilled in precept and proverb, and then cast . . . into the mould of a comprehensive educational programme for future generations' (Aitken 1986: 4).

The teacher, then, does not speak by personal authority alone, but he is also the voice of the received tradition that transcends him (Lang 1986: 37). Over time, transmitted wisdom was verified, adjusted, augmented and supported by subsequent observation of life. The curriculum, therefore, was not static, but dynamic, as the insights of generations of sages progressively coalesced into a more coherent philosophy (Clements 1992: 44).

The paucity of references in the biblical wisdom literature to matters distinctive to Israel suggests that the wisdom teachers searched for universal insights about life. Because their worldview was based upon the premise that Yahweh is the sole creator and sovereign of the world, they 'acknowledged no geographical boundaries where insight into reality was concerned' (Crenshaw 1981a: 79). Of course, any borrowings from other cultures would need to be reinterpreted in the light of the worldview of Israel before they could be included in the corpus

---

[6] Farmer (1991: 43) correctly points out that the sexual language in this passage is used elsewhere of religious apostasy against Yahweh, as for example in Jeremiah 2:13. Nevertheless, as Whybray (1994b: 89) argues, the use of the figure of a well of living water in Song of Songs 4:15 for sexual pleasure is a more likely parallel. Though both sexual and religious fidelity are in view in Proverbs 1 – 9, in 5:15–20 the literal aspect of sexual intimacy is at the forefront.

of received tradition,[7] but there was no presumptive bias against observations derived from other cultures.

The Bible refers to wise men in several ancient Near Eastern cultures, including Egypt (Gn. 41:8; Ex. 7:11; Is. 19:11–12), Babylon (Is. 44:25; Je. 50:35; 51:57) and Persia (Est. 1:13; 6:13). In both Egypt and Mesopotamia wisdom was centred in royal schools, in which numerous literary works were developed to assist in the education of courtiers and scribes (Crenshaw 1981a: 55). The extensive political links between Israel and Egypt, especially from the time of Solomon onwards, might suggest that biblical wisdom was heavily dependent on the antecedent tradition in Egypt. In fact, aside from formal features such as the address 'my son', and a few prominent parallels such as Proverbs 22:17 – 24:22 and the Egyptian Instruction of Amenemope,[8] the book of Proverbs, and especially Proverbs 1 – 9, manifests relatively little dependence upon the wisdom of Egypt. The purported correspondence between order and the Egyptian concept of *Maat* has been questioned by more recent study (see pages 28–30). The biblical teachers of wisdom are aware of comparable discussions in the surrounding cultures, and at times they make use of images, concepts and even literary texts from those cultures, but the body of knowledge that they compose is rooted distinctively in the Yahwistic worldview.[9]

---

[7] *Cf.* von Rad (1972: 317): 'To a greater extent than is the case in any other intellectual or religious sphere, Israel's wisdom has borrowed from neighbouring cultures. Indeed, she perhaps first learned, through her familiarity with foreign wisdom, to see correctly the real importance of many of the basic human questions. But what she borrowed she incorporated into the sphere of a belief in God and an understanding of reality which were different from those of her neighbours. Thus Israel had to accomplish this task faced both with unique opportunities and with unique difficulties. Unique, too, was her confidence that she could recognize God's ways in the world around her as well as the limitations she encountered in this task.'

[8] Walton (1989: 192–197) analyses the parallel texts and concludes: 'In the end, it cannot be denied that Israelite wisdom shares much with the wisdom of Egypt, and there is no reason to doubt or deny that the Israelites were aware of and influenced by Egyptian literature. Whatever the amount of this general indebtedness, it has not yet been demonstrated that any specific Israelite work was merely an adaptation of any specific Egyptian work' (1989: 196–197).

[9] Clements (1992: 17) assesses the data fairly: 'We can accept that, with appropriate local variations, the search for wisdom and understanding was a very widespread feature of the nations and cities that emerged in the ancient Near East from as far back as the fourth millennium BCE. To what extent this

Proverbs 1 – 9 includes several references to tradition transmitted to the learner by an authority figure. On two occasions the instruction of both father and mother is cited, strongly suggesting that the knowledge is received from the learner's physical parents:

> Listen, my son, to your father's instruction·
> and do not forsake your mother's teaching (1:8).

> My son, keep your father's commands
> and do not forsake your mother's teaching (6:20).

As Deuteronomy 21:18–19 indicates, both parents were involved in the instruction and discipline of the child. Though in ancient Israel education doubtless was nurtured in several contexts, including the court and the clan, the family was also a crucial component in the overall process of learning. McKane (1970: 268) observes:

> The home is a primary educational agency, and it is there that the foundations of civilized behaviour and general excellence are laid. The son who learns from his parents is already beginning to lose his rawness and to present a pleasing presence to the world.

It is likely that only a small portion of the youth in Israel would have had the leisure and means to be educated outside the home (Aitken 1986: 53). The knowledge received from parents, therefore, was the cognitive foundation for the learner, for it oriented him to life through the transmission of observations mediated through the father and the mother.[10]

---

feature of ancient civilization passed directly from one community to another, and how far it displayed the marks of parallel quests emerging among different groups, is not wholly clear. Certainly there are abundant indications that the search for such wisdom and its application to daily life represented a significant feature that accompanied the spread of urban civilization from the time of the rise of Sumerian power.'

[10] Crenshaw (1985: 614) concludes: '. . . the bulk of education may very well have taken place in the family setting, where practical instruction in daily life was provided for boys and girls according to the opportunities open to them. Guilds of various kinds probably broadened the clientele beyond the immediate family while narrowing the scope of learning.'

Proverbs 1 – 9, however, appears to derive from outside the home. The repeated address, 'My son', parallels the custom in other ancient Near Eastern cultures of referring to the teacher-learner relationship in the language of father and son. In the biblical literature the schools of the prophets employ this expression, for the prophet is called 'father' (2 Ki. 2:12), and the apprentices who serve him are called 'the company [$b^e n\hat{e}$ = sons] of the prophets' (2 Ki. 2:3, 5, 7, 15).

The teacher of wisdom presents to the learner instruction validated by experience. McKane (1970: 303) remarks:

> It is the accumulated sagacity of many generations to whose value the father or teacher can personally testify. He derives his authority from the circumstance that he is in a good succession; because he has lived inside the tradition and allowed it to shape his life, he can speak with a personal and not merely a derivative authority.

In Proverbs 7:6–23 the teacher describes his observation of the devastating fall of a young man to the enticement of a promiscuous woman. On the basis of what he has seen, he then exhorts the learner to listen to his counsel (7:24–27). On another occasion (4:3–4), the teacher refers to knowledge that he received from his own teacher or father, which he is now transmitting to the student. This knowledge, received either through personal observation or by the testimony of another authority, serves as the basis for the teacher's repeated challenges to the youth to accept his words (2:1; 3:1; 4:2, 10, 20; 5:1, 7). Through this approach the teacher encourages reception of the tradition, which is reliable knowledge, rather than independent investigation by the learner, which is more susceptible to error. The greater experience of the teacher is the rationale for submitting to his authority and accepting what he says as true.

Revelation

Proverbs 1 – 9 also demonstrates that there is knowledge that is not observable by humans, but has been revealed by Yahweh. Unlike the historical and prophetic texts of the Old Testament with their frequent explicit references to Yahweh's revelatory works and words, the wisdom writings typically assume revelation as an implicit axiom that undergirds human observation as a source of knowledge (Cox 1993: 15; Goldingay 1979: 194). In the wisdom tradition there is a sense of mystery, for some things are known only to Yahweh. Though he has set much knowledge within the range of human observation, some elements of truth are knowable only because he himself reveals them by means that transcend direct human investigation.

Proverbs 2:6 teaches that Yahweh is the ultimate source of wisdom, knowledge and understanding: 'For the LORD gives wisdom, and from his mouth come knowledge and understanding.' As personified wisdom declares in Proverbs 8:22–31, wisdom is the eternal possession of Yahweh. In light of Yahweh's exhaustive knowledge, the learner is charged to trust in Yahweh with all his heart rather than leaning on his own understanding (3:5). Greenstone (1950: 27) comments:

> Human understanding is not always reliable and has to look for support to divine guidance. Understanding is important and one should make every effort to attain it, but one should not rely on it entirely, since experience has shown that it is fallible and has to have divine support.

Revelation as a source for knowledge is demonstrated by the references to creation. By definition, the creation of the world by Yahweh occurred beyond the range of human observation. Proverbs 3:19–20 states:

> By wisdom the LORD laid the earth's foundations,
>   by understanding he set the heavens in place;
> by his knowledge the deeps were divided,
>   and the clouds let drop the dew.

This revelatory statement gives the divine eyewitness account of the origin of the world and of the place of wisdom within Yahweh's universe. The world is depicted as the immediate creation of Yahweh. Wisdom, though bearing authority over humans, 'is from the very beginning inferior to and dependent on Yahweh, a tool in his hands' (Whybray 1994b: 68).

The more extensive statement concerning creation in

Proverbs 8:22–31 also reveals that the world came into being with designed order by the direct creative activity of Yahweh. Greater emphasis, however, is placed on the role of wisdom, who was the nursling at his side who delighted in the presence of Yahweh and in the world which he created. As Whybray (1994b: 128) argues persuasively, the monotheism of Israel's faith is supported by the portrayal in Proverbs 8:22–31 of the creation of the world as the exclusive act of Yahweh. He observes:

> The tone is already set by the change of subject at the beginning: the name of Yahweh stands there as the very first word and in an emphatic position . . . This emphasis is continued by means of further verbs of which he is the subject in vv. 26, 27, 28, 29, Wisdom's status or presence being defined in relation to these creative acts (vv. 25, 27, 30–31). Wisdom, in other words, is not engaged here in any independent activity or indeed as having any independent existence before, during or even after the acts of creation are performed: it is in Yahweh's inhabited world (v. 31) that she rejoices.

The creation of the world, then, is a component in the curriculum of education that is known solely because it has been revealed by Yahweh, not because it has been discovered by human observation.

The fear of Yahweh, which has already been examined as a key value and goal in education, is also relevant to the knowledge base for education. Proverbs 1:7, which serves as the thesis statement for Proverbs 1 – 9, states: 'The fear of the LORD is the beginning of knowledge, but fools despise wisdom and discipline.' McKane (1970: 264) remarks:

> The acquisition of knowledge and wisdom does not now depend on a severe educational discipline in which submission is made to the authority of a teacher and the pupil's attitudes formed by his assimilation of a body of traditional, empirically based wisdom.

Neither the autonomy of personal observation nor the authority of tradition mediated through the teacher is the ultimate or comprehensive source of knowledge. Instead, the learner must acknowledge Yahweh as the omniscient deity, and accept with reverence the knowledge that he reveals.

Because Yahweh is the sole deity who knows everything, all knowledge ultimately is related to him. Proverbs 1:29–30, therefore, demonstrates a close connection between the fear of Yahweh and wisdom. Personified wisdom describes the fools as those who 'hated knowledge and did not choose to fear the LORD' (1:29), but then continues to say, 'they would not accept my advice and spurned my rebuke' (1:30). By rejecting the knowledge and insight available through wisdom, they are at the same time rejecting Yahweh's knowledge. In a comparable way, an insistence on personal autonomy in defining wisdom, rather than fearing Yahweh, is condemned in Proverbs 3:7.

Conclusion

In Proverbs 1 – 9 the content base, or curriculum, for education is drawn from three sources. One passage, Proverbs 6:6–8, points to direct observation of the physical environment. In Proverbs 5:15–20 the learner is directed to personal observation of the satisfaction of sexual intimacy in marriage as a preventative against the allurement of the strange woman.

The predominant source of knowledge in Proverbs 1 – 9 is mediated through tradition communicated by the teacher. The initial section of Proverbs does not draw extensively from the parallel wisdom traditions of Egypt and Mesopotamia. Instead, the parent or, more commonly, the teacher transmits to the learner what he has personally observed or what he himself has received by the testimony of another authority. The knowledge base for education, then, is determined by the superior experience of the teacher.

In addition to observation and tradition, divine revelation also contributes to the curriculum for education in Proverbs 1 – 9. In particular, references to creation presuppose the communication of facts that are directly knowable only to God. The correlation between the fear of Yahweh and wisdom shows that knowledge in its total dimensions finds its ultimate source in him.

Though knowledge may be acquired through various means, by personal observation, traditional instruction or divine revelation, there is a basic unity of truth which finds its ultimate source in the omniscient Yahweh. The curriculum for education, then, encompasses the whole range of knowledge that Yahweh has made known, whether immediately by his revelation, or mediately through teachers transmitting tradition, or through personal observation by the learner.

Chapter Five

Process of instruction

Instruction comprises the ways in which a teacher uses curriculum in the process of educating the learner. The effective teacher employs strategies by which the learner can acquire the knowledge, competence, character and attitudes that are desired.

Even a cursory glance at Proverbs 1 – 9 reveals that the teacher uses a wide variety of instructional techniques, including 'direct appeals for attention, rhetorical questions, extended metaphors approaching allegory, vivid description, anecdote' (Crenshaw 1981a: 73; *cf.* McKane 1970: 7). In the prologue, the author states that the teachers of wisdom instruct through proverbs, parables, sayings and riddles (Pr. 1:6). Crenshaw (1981a: 32) elucidates the distinctive strategies implicit in each of these techniques:

> . . . the proverb (*mašal*) refers to a basic similitude or likeness, wherein a given phenomenon is set alongside another as illuminating it in some significant fashion . . . The second word, parable (*mᵉliṣah*), seems to point in the direction of sayings which carry a sting hidden within their clever formulation, and may by extension refer to admonitions and warnings. The expression 'wise sayings' seems to function as a sort of general category, and consequently serves to identify certain collections within the present book of Proverbs. The final word, riddles (*ḥidoth*), designates enigmatic sayings and perhaps even extensive reflections on the meaning of life and its inequities.

In Proverbs 1 – 9 multiple strategies are used by the teacher in the process of instructing the learner.

The various rhetorical devices are not simply for the sake of variety. Instead, the process of instruction always serves the purpose of instruction, for the teacher creates a strategy that makes wisdom compelling for the learner. As a result, 'the teachings of the sages evoked the imagination, provided insight into faith and morality, stimulated critical reflection, and became the basis for rational decision making and moral action' (Perdue 1994: 50).

The teacher uses language to great effect in instructing the learner. Consequently, appreciating the rhetorical devices that are employed in Proverbs 1 – 9 is essential if one is to discern how the teacher influences the student. Moreover, how the teacher instructs the learner will play a primary role in determining the roles of both the teacher and the learner in the implicit pedagogical theory of Proverbs 1 – 9 (cf. chapters 6 and 7).

This section, in keeping with nearly the entire corpus of biblical wisdom, is composed as poetry. An essential feature of poetry is that it endeavours to re-create experience, rather than merely reporting it. Its artful use of compressed language does more than inform the hearers of facts; it leads to meditation and pondering as the hearer gradually assimilates the multi-dimensional meaning.[1] A key component of poetry is meta-phorical language. Not only does the extensive use of figures of speech create the attractive quality of elegance and beauty (Perdue 1994: 63–64), but it also makes abstract concepts concrete, and therefore more accessible to the learner. Mouser (1983: 86) observes:

> Because figures of speech arise for the most part from concrete nouns and verbs, they draw upon a world of sensory experience, real or imagined, through which

[1] Craigie (1979: 9) develops this point: '. . . the educational system seems to depend heavily on a particular understanding of the human memory and of the role for the subconscious mind in the moral life and the decision-making process. The substance of the Book of Proverbs is, for the most part, poetic in form. And the statements of wisdom are memorable, not merely by virtue of their brevity, but by virtue of their poetic structure. They are designed to be memorized, designed to bring out their moral truth powerfully. They sink from the conscious mind of the student to the subconscious mind of the adult in later years, only to be recalled to the conscious mind later in life at each moment of moral decision.'

even abstract ideas can be communicated. The vivid-
ness of many figures of speech aids in communication
in two important ways. First, figures of speech enable a
speaker to express strange, abstract or unknown ideas
in terms of known experience. Second, figures of
speech help to hold the attention of a reader or
listeners, assuring full communication.

The book of Proverbs derives its name from the *mᵉšālîm* which
constitute its characteristic mode of expression. The *mᵉšālîm* use
comparisons to inspire, encourage and challenge the learner
(O'Conner 1988: 37). Exploiting the full range of relationships
possible between the two points of comparison,[2] proverbs at
times illuminate the learner, and at other times use ambiguity
and enigma to tease the learner into deeper understanding. As
O'Conner (1988: 20) notes, the teacher is employing a
conscious instructional strategy: 'The point of highlighting
ambiguity or paradox is not to bring the individual to an
intellectual impasse but to lead her beyond the obvious into
deeper, transcendent truth.'
Although much of the curriculum for education in Proverbs
1 – 9 represents tradition transmitted from the teacher to the
learner, the instructional strategies do not just compel unquestioning acceptance (Perdue 1993: 74). Rather than demanding
compliance based solely on the authority of the teacher, wisdom
frequently directs by indirection. The comparisons posed by the
proverbs serve as implicit exhortations as they set in antithesis
the wise way with its beneficent results and the foolish way with
its disastrous consequences. The teacher places concrete
observations from life before the learner, challenging the
learner to infer the principle which they teach. Melchert (1990:
371) concludes: 'Pedagogically, that practice suggests that the
listener or reader be an active participant or an interpreter, and
not just a passive recipient of another's wisdom. The listener can
help create the wisdom.' In addition, the teacher frequently

---

[2] Scott (1965: 5–8) lists seven kinds of patterns found in Proverbs: (1) identity,
equivalence, invariable associations; (2) non-identity, contrast, paradox; (3)
similarity, analogy, type; (4) contrary to right order = futile, absurd; (5)
classifies, characterizes persons, actions or situations; (6) value, relative value or
priority, proportion, degree; and (7) consequences of human character and
behaviour.

provides a rationale for the instructions he gives, thus involving the learner in the process of thinking through the issues for himself (Cox 1993: 12).

Instruction, then, is designed not to bring about the desired behaviours by coercive force, but to guide the learner into choosing to follow the wise way. As an analysis of the rhetoric of pedagogy in Proverbs 1 – 9 will reveal, the teacher uses a wide range of strategies as he instructs the learner. This chapter will investigate the diverse rhetorical forms used in Proverbs 1 – 9, beginning with the most directive utterances and proceeding toward more non-directive sayings.

Address

In Proverbs 1:20–33 and 8:1–11 personified wisdom assumes the role of a teacher who addresses prospective learners. In each of the passages wisdom as the teacher initiates the learning process by confronting people in the gate of the city (1:20–21; 8:1–3). At this strategic location wisdom appeals to all humans to listen to her words. As Whybray (1994b: 45) notes, 'by making her appeal in public she reaches the widest possible audience, and also asserts her relevance to the mundane reality of the market place.' The teacher is not content to wait until the learner shows interest, but wisdom seeks the places where human activity is busiest, and then she raises her voice in bold address as she seeks a hearing.[3]

In wisdom's first address, she uses two rhetorical questions to elicit attention: 'How long will you simple ones love your simple ways? How long will mockers delight in mockery and fools hate knowledge?' (Pr. 1:22). She follows these questions with a conditional statement which points out that wisdom alone is

---

[3] McKane (1970: 345) notes well: 'She operates where the competition is fiercest, not so much the competition of other orators as men's preoccupation with those things which they take more seriously than listening to speeches – earning their living, making bargains, getting wealth, transacting local politics, settling disputes and other less deliberate gregarious enjoyments. It is against all this that Wisdom has to compete, raising her voice and summoning an audience until she wins one by the sustained force of her eloquence. She picks a place where human traffic is heaviest, whether on a natural pulpit at the side of the road or at a cross-roads or beside the gates which give access to the city, where there is a continual movement to and fro and where the forum on which all manner of public transactions focus is located.'

the source of insight (1:23). Wisdom has much to offer the learner, if only he will respond to her.

Using the tone of a prophet, wisdom uses accusations and threats of judgment in an effort to shake the learners from their simplicity, mocking and folly. Though the teacher uses the language of wisdom in charging that 'you ignored all my advice and would not accept my rebuke' (1:25), the style used is reminiscent of prophetic denunciation with its threats of disaster (Whybray 1994: 43; Crenshaw 1981a: 96). Because wisdom has been ignored heretofore, she will deride the calamity of those who mocked her (1:26–27). Though they turn to wisdom in their distress, they will find that wisdom must be found on its terms (1:28). The tragedy is that in rejecting the teaching of wisdom humans are refusing to fear Yahweh (1:29), and that will lead inevitably to destruction (1:30–32).

On the other hand, wisdom does extend the prospect of hope, for she concludes her address in Proverbs 1:33: '. . . but whoever listens to me will live in safety and be at ease, without fear of harm.' Wisdom is an authoritative teacher who must be heard and obeyed (McKane 1970: 276). In this address she calls for receptive submission to what she teaches, and she threatens disaster for those who refuse to listen to her instruction.

The address in Proverbs 8:1–11 is part of a longer unit comprising chapter 8 which uses several instructional strategies. As in Proverbs 1:20–33, wisdom takes the initiative to meet people where they are in the marketplace of life. Her call, however, is not just addressed to the simple and the foolish (8:5), but she raises her voice to all humanity (8:4).

The prominent feature in this address is wisdom's self-recommendation, 'in which she boasts of her power and authority and of the gifts which she is able to bestow' (Whybray 1994b: 119).[4] Wisdom as the teacher claims that she speaks what

---

[4] Whybray goes on to observe: 'This is a speech by a supernatural being in praise of herself. It is reminiscent of a widespread literary genre attested in Egyptian, Sumerian, Babylonian and other Near Eastern religious texts in which a divinity, frequently a goddess (Maat, Isis, Astarte/Ishtar and many others) praises herself. In the Old Testament too Yahweh occasionally speaks in praise of himself (notably in Isa. 42:8–9; 44:24–8; 45:5–7), but the contents of his speeches are quite unlike those of Wisdom's speech here. It seems probable that some of the imagery of self-praise in Prov. 8 has been shaped by literary conventions derived from polytheism; but, whatever polytheistic connections

is right and just (8:6–8). Those who possess discernment will recognize that her teaching is plain and straightforward (8:9; *cf.* Whybray 1994b: 123). She calls upon her hearers to choose her instruction instead of material riches, because no human desire can compare with the benefits of wisdom (8:10–11).

In the two examples of address which have been examined, the teacher initiates the learning process by calling to potential learners in the context of their everyday lives. Wisdom challenges her hearers to listen, not to dialogue. By threatening disaster on those who refuse to listen, and by describing her impeccable credentials as a reliable teacher, wisdom calls the learner to receptive submission to her authoritative instruction. The rhetorical form of address contains virtually no reference to active learner participation in the learning process. What is at the forefront is the authoritative utterance of the eminently qualified teacher.

Description

The second rhetorical strategy used in Proverbs 1 – 9 is description that teaches without explicit reference to explanation, rationale or illustration. The two examples in Proverbs 6:12–19 and 8:22–31 are in effect lectures by experts that are intended to be heard and understood by the learner. No doubt there is an implied expectation that the learner will draw some kind of conclusion from the knowledge which he hears, but the descriptions themselves do not elicit a response. The primary stance of this form of instruction is that of the knowledgeable authority.

Proverbs 6:12–19 contains two complementary portraits of the evil person and the evil activities which Yahweh hates:

> A scoundrel and villain,
>> who goes about with a corrupt mouth,
>> who winks with his eye,
>> signals with his feet

this text may have had in an earlier form, the chapter in its present form is monotheistic. Wisdom is intended to be understood as an attribute or heavenly servant of the sole God Yahweh to whom he has delegated certain powers with regard to his relations with mankind' (1994b: 119–120).

and motions with his fingers,
who plots evil with deceit in his heart –
he always stirs up dissension.
Therefore disaster will overtake him in an instant;
he will suddenly be destroyed – without remedy.

There are six things the LORD hates,
seven that are detestable to him:
haughty eyes,
a lying tongue,
hands that shed innocent blood,
a heart that devises wicked schemes,
feet that are quick to rush into evil,
a false witness who pours out lies
and a man who stirs up dissension among brothers.

By using a numerical sequence, the teacher endeavours to define the order implicit in Yahweh's world (Nel 1982: 11).[5] The common feature that ties together the traits listed in this passage is disruptive, self-assertive behaviour that rejects Yahweh's values, and which is therefore rejected by him (McKane 1970: 326). Of course, this list is illustrative, not exhaustive, but its selections elucidate for the learner the kind of behaviour which must be avoided. What should be noted, however, is that the teacher does not make a specific appeal to the learner, but he gives words of description without explicit direction.

Proverbs 8:22–31 consists of a self-description by personified wisdom. In establishing its credibility as an authority to be heard and heeded, wisdom describes its relationship to Yahweh and its antiquity. These two factors are emphasized, so that the learner will become disposed to accept and obey the instructions of wisdom. In this passage 'Wisdom justifies her claims and the

---

[5] Von Rad (1972: 35) notes that this effort to systematize observations of life is also found in other ancient Near Eastern cultures: 'The counting and listing of things, of types of behaviour, of virtues, etc., is an elementary need of man in his search for order. This can be amply attested in many different forms in every culture. In the case of the so-called numerical saying it is with this desire for order, planted deep within man, that we have to do, particularly in a quite specific form of proverb which was cultivated not only in Israel but also in other lands of the ancient Near East and which has increasingly attracted the interest of scholars.'

veracity of her words by her antiquity, by her station next to God when he ordered the world for humanity, and by her indispensable mediation between God and that humanity' (Yee 1989: 63).

Wisdom describes its antiquity from before the creation of the world in Proverbs 8:22–26:

> The LORD brought me forth as the first of his works,
>   before his deeds of old;
> I was appointed from eternity,
>   from the beginning, before the world began.
> When there were no oceans, I was given birth,
>   when there were no springs abounding with water;
> before the mountains were settled in place,
>   before the hills, I was given birth,
> before he made the earth or its fields
>   or any of the dust of the world.

The fact that Yahweh appointed wisdom from eternity indicates that from the first it had an honoured status in his design. Throughout the whole creation of the world, wisdom was with Yahweh, observing with delight how he crafted the universe, including humanity:

> I was there when he set the heavens in place,
>   when he marked out the horizon on the face of the
>   deep,
> when he established the clouds above
>   and fixed securely the fountains of the deep,
> when he gave the sea its boundary
>   so the waters would not overstep his command,
> and when he marked out the foundations of the earth.
>   Then I was the craftsman at his side.
> I was filled with delight day after day,
>   rejoicing always in his presence,
> rejoicing in his whole world
>   and delighting in mankind (8:27–31).

As already discussed on page 24, the term *'āmôn* in 8:30 is best rendered 'nursling'. Unlike the statement in Proverbs 3:19, 'By wisdom the LORD laid the earth's foundations,' Proverbs 8:22–

31 does not describe wisdom as an active participant in creation but as a delighted spectator of Yahweh's work.[6] Nevertheless, wisdom's ancient origin and its proximity to Yahweh establish it as a reliable authority for life. Though the description does not draw the conclusion, the implication for the learner is clear: it would be foolhardy to neglect the principles taught by this longstanding and well-connected teacher.

Condition with command

In Proverbs 6:1–5 a set of conditions is followed by explicit words of command:

> My son, if you have put up security for your neighbour,
> if you have struck hands in pledge for another,
> if you have been trapped by what you said,
> ensnared by the words of your mouth,
> then do this, my son, to free yourself,
> since you have fallen into your neighbour's hands:
> Go and humble yourself;
> press your plea with your neighbour!
> Allow no sleep to your eyes,
> no slumber to your eyelids.
> Free yourself, like a gazelle from the hand of the hunter,
> like a bird from the snare of the fowler.

---

[6] Whybray (1994b: 135) argues cogently: 'For the purposes of the interpretation of the poem as a whole the crucial question is obviously whether Wisdom is here seen as actively participating in the creation of the world or simply as a spectator whose mere presence there gives her eminent status. It is significant that nowhere else in the poem is there any suggestion of such constructive activity on her part (unless her "building a house" 9:1; 14:1 is interpreted in cosmic terms). However the verbs in vv. 22–6 are interpreted, she is not credited there with any form of activity; and in relation to the acts of creation described in vv. 27–30a Wisdom only says of herself "I was there" (v. 27) and "I was beside him" (v. 30). In vv. 30–31 she merely delights in the world that God has made. *Master workman*, then, as referring to Wisdom, seems out of place. The interpretations of later Jewish exegetes, and the explicit statement in the Wisdom of Solomon that Wisdom made all things – a view which is *not* held by Ben Sira (Sir. 1: 24) – do not constitute evidence for the original intention of this author: they merely show that Prov 8:22–31 was the starting-point for later theological speculation.'

The teacher sets forth a set of circumstances in which a person's misguided generosity in pledging his financial resources as security for a neighbour risks his own impoverishment. As Scott (1965: 58) observes, this well-intentioned commitment could reduce one to abject poverty or even slavery. Though the Mosaic law encouraged mutual financial support within the covenant community, Proverbs contain numerous warnings against generosity becoming a self-inflicted trap.[7] The one who has committed himself unwisely must humble himself if necessary as he importunes his neighbour to release him from the obligation. Like an animal that has been cornered or ensnared, he must make every effort to extricate himself.[8]

The use of conditions to introduce commands is a pattern typical of the Egyptian Instruction texts as well. As McKane (1970: 76) observes, 'the function of the conditional clause is to define the condition or circumstances in which the imperative(s) applies.' This rhetorical form is highly directive, for if the learner falls within the parameters of the condition, then the command necessarily applies. The teacher offers no reason to justify the command, but merely an observation of the existing and potential situation confronting the learner. If the learner meets the stated conditions, then he is obligated to obey the authoritative directives of the teacher.

[7] Whybray (1994b: 94) gives a useful discussion on the danger of providing security for a loan in the biblical culture: 'Other passages in Proverbs on the same theme (11:15; 17:18; 20:16; 22:26–7; 27:13) help to some extent to fill out the picture. In particular, 22:27 shows that the pledge in question is a financial one: if the person on whose half [sic] the guarantee has been made defaults or is unable to pay, the amount pledged will become due. To give such guarantees in a moment of pity or generosity, therefore, is folly (17:18). It puts the guarantor into the power of the creditor (6:3), who may then seek to recoup his losses by distraining his goods (22:27) or even enslaving him or his family (compare 2 Kg 4:1–7). Throughout Proverbs the likelihood of such a disaster is thought to be so great that, although giving to the poor out of one's resources is strongly encouraged in several passages in the sentence literature, standing surety is equally forcefully and unconditionally condemned as an act of folly.'

[8] Zornberg (1982: 58) comments: 'The gazelle can save itself from the trap by sheer bodily force, while the bird can flutter its wings so desperately in the clutch of the snare that some of its feathers are plucked out and it can then fly off free. So the pupil is advised to gain release either by sheer physical labor and toil, or by "shedding" externals, such as clothing, money, or valuables, to placate his creditor.'

Command with reasons

The largest single category of rhetoric in Proverbs 1 – 9 comprises commands supported with reasons. The commands may be either positive admonitions or negative prohibitions[9] which are followed by reasons introduced by a variety of particles or by other comparable grammatical constructions (Nel 1982: 68–69). In the attempt to make their commands clear and compelling, the teachers of wisdom use many kinds of motivation. In Proverbs 1 – 9 most of the motivations are appeals to observation and reason, because wisdom is predicated on a worldview which holds that Yahweh created the world as an ordered universe. Consequently, 'the wisdom expressed in the admonition represents the created order in which one's existence finds its destiny' (Nel 1982: 91).

The use of reasons with commands is highly significant for defining how the teacher approaches the learner. As McKane (1970: 78) explains well,

> . . . the authoritative aspect of the teaching is strongly emphasized, but care is taken to show that there are good reasons why the teaching can be inculcated with such assurance. In bulk the argument at least matches the imperatives, and the formal arrangement may be taken as an indication that there is an intrinsic balance between authority and reasonableness.

Rather than demanding compliance based only upon the authority of the teacher, commands bolstered by reasons direct the learner toward right thinking. In doing this, the teacher brings the learner face to face with the issue at hand. Without insisting that the learner submit to an unsubstantiated authoritative dictum, the teacher gives direction, but then places the responsibility upon the learner to act reasonably. Melchert (1992: 150) concludes:

---

[9] Perdue (1994: 67–68) distinguishes between these two forms of command: 'Admonitions are imperatives that attempt to persuade the hearer to engage in a course of action or to embody a particular virtue. Prohibitions are imperatives plus a negative ("no," "not"), designed to dissuade the hearer from taking a course of action or from embodying some sort of vice or foolishness.'

The ways of the sages demand that a teacher respect the learner and his or her own experience and readiness to hear. This does not deny the teacher's authority, for the learner must also respect experience and insight, where the teacher's authority is grounded. This approach to teaching expects *the learner* to be the primary actor, not the teacher. The learner must see – the teacher cannot do the seeing for the learner.

Instruction, then, is viewed as a synergism, with both the teacher and the learner playing crucial roles.

Proverbs 3:1–12 contains six commands paired with corresponding reasons.[10] The first five reasons all relate to the personal prosperity which the learner will receive as a result of keeping the commands. The final reason in Proverbs 3:12 supports the prohibition against despising Yahweh's discipline and resenting his rebuke by arguing that divine discipline is the evidence of Yahweh's parental love.[11] Ross (1991: 918) observes, 'This motivation recalls the language of the Davidic covenant (2 Sam 7:14; Ps 89:32–33), which mentions discipline in love. Indeed, it is the father-son relationship that provides insight into the nature of that discipline.' The motivation for the learner's response to the teacher's commands is the recognition that this way is advantageous to him, and that Yahweh's discipline is a demonstration of divine love. It is in the learner's best interests to submit to the directions of the teacher.

Proverbs 4:10–19 sets before the learner two ways, the path of

---

[10] McKane (1970: 289–290) details the form of Proverbs 3:1–12: 'With regard to vv. 1–12, the imperative (or jussive) appears in vv. 1, 3, 5, 7, 9, 11. In v. 1 a negative imperative and a jussive are arranged antithetically and are recommended by a motive clause which explains why they should be attended to (v. 2). Then a negative jussive, followed by two imperatives, leads on to a consequential clause (vv. 3–4). Similarly, vv. 5f. contain three imperatives and a consequential clause, as also vv. 7f. In vv. 9f., a single imperative is followed by two consequential clauses, and in vv. 11f. two imperatives are reinforced by a motive clause.'

[11] Whybray (1994b: 65) discusses the absence of a verb in 3:12b: 'LXX has a verb here; and the very similar passage in Job (5:18) has *yak'ib*, "he inflicts pain". Emendation to a form of this verb – *e.g.* the piel *(wᵉ)kē'ēb*, yielding the line "and he inflicts suffering on the son in which he delights" – would be syntactically an improvement, and would still preserve the "father-son" analogy. However, MT may be correct.'

wisdom and the path of the wicked. In the wisdom literature, and particularly in Proverbs, the metaphor of the path or way, *derek*, is a familiar image for the course of life (Koch, *TDOT* III: 271–272).[12] The *derek* speaks of ordered, purposive movement in a single direction (Habel 1972: 137). According to biblical wisdom the path of wisdom leads to life in its fullness, but the path of folly leads to death in all of its dimensions. Whybray (1994b: 78–79) summarizes the significance of the image of the two ways in this passage:

> It affirms human freedom to make a choice about the conduct of one's life, and sets out the inevitable consequences of these two 'ways of life', that of righteousness and that of wickedness. There is apparently no middle way, and no possibility of changing course is mentioned: it seems to be taken for granted that the choice once made stamps the character indelibly. A strong pressure is thus put on the pupil to choose now, and to choose rightly and wisely.

The teacher states that the way of wisdom which he recommends leads to pleasurable progress[13] in life (4:10–12), so the learner should hold on to the instruction he has received (4:13). In 4:14–15 the teacher cautions against the path of the wicked, for it is the way which destroys character (4:16–17). The final verses of the passage contrast the path of the righteous which leads to full light (4:18) with the way of the wicked which is like deep darkness (4:19). This concluding antithesis points implicitly to the need for the learner to decide to choose wisdom as the teacher has instructed.

The rhetorical technique of commands with reasons is also used in Proverbs 4:20–27. This passage is especially weighted

---

[12] Bergman (*TDOT* III: 274) cites several examples from the Egyptian wisdom literature that parallel the usage of the biblical image of the way of life or the way of God.

[13] Aitken (1986: 56) expounds the metaphor in Proverbs 4:12: '"Hampered" is literally "narrow, cramped". In Isaiah 49:19–20 the word is used of cramped living conditions, the lack of living space in the land resulting from a population explosion. So then, there is plenty of leg room on this road to take firm, even strides. Indeed, the traveller can break into a run without fear of taking a tumble.'

toward commands, with reasons represented only in verses 22 and 23b. The image of the path of life is alluded to in verses 25–27, but it is not developed into a clear statement of the two ways, as in Proverbs 4:10–19. The learner is challenged to align each area of his life, represented by the sensory organs, with what is right. Above all, the learner is advised to guard his heart, the wellspring of life (4:23), by keeping the teacher's words within it (4:20–21). Careful appropriation of teaching, then, will equip the learner to function correctly throughout the full range of life's activities (Cohen 1952: 24).

The admonition against involvement with the adulteress in Proverbs 5:7–23 employs reasons to support the warning. In 5:9–14 the high price in personal loss is a mirror image of the blessings poured out by wisdom (3:13–18). As Aitken (1986: 63) summarizes:

> In short, he is a destroyed man – personally and socially. He loses every shred of dignity and the respect of his neighbours (v. 9); wastes all his resources – material, physical and mental (vv. 10–11); is filled with remorse when he learns too late how foolish he has been (vv. 12–13), and is exposed to public disgrace (v. 14).

The succeeding strophe, Proverbs 5:15–23, recommends the enjoyment of sexual delights within the boundaries of marriage as an antidote against the allurements of the adulteress (5:15–19). With this source of legitimate pleasure available, the teacher poses two rhetorical questions calculated to press the learner to consider carefully his decision in the face of temptation: 'Why be captivated, my son, by an adulteress? Why embrace the bosom of another man's wife?' (5:20). As further incentive to choose the wise course of action, the teacher reminds the learner that human acts are in the full view of Yahweh (5:21).[14] Furthermore, rejecting the discipline of

---

[14] Aitken (1986: 66) remarks insightfully: 'So far in this chapter the sage has appealed for a prudent weighing up of the consequences as a deterrent against becoming involved with loose women: it is simply not worth it, for there is everything to lose and nothing to gain. In verse 21, however, he shifts into a higher gear. While the foolish man may take steps to hide his sordid affair from the eyes of others (7:9; *cf.* Job 24:15) and may put all thought of God out of his

wisdom leads into sin which enslaves. If the learner desires true pleasure, real freedom and God's approval, then he should heed the counsel of the teacher.

The lengthy call by personified wisdom in Proverbs 8 concludes with a final appeal to the learners to listen to her (8:32a, 33). Great blessings await those who attend to wisdom (8:32b, 34), described in general terms as life and favour from Yahweh (8:35). On the other hand, wisdom says, 'But whoever fails to find me harms himself; all who hate me love death' (8:36). Clearly, the choice is left to the learner, but the teacher has defined the two alternatives and the consequences to which each leads.

In contrast to most of Proverbs 1 – 9, which is typically addressed directly to the learner, Proverbs 9:7–12 employs a more indirect form of rhetoric. The teacher declares that some people are unteachable mockers (9:7–8a) who 'resist all attempts to educate them, not only because of intellectual but also because of moral obtuseness' (McKane 1970: 368). The wise person, however, welcomes instruction (9:9).[15] Wisdom promises rewards, including long life, to those who receive it (9:11–12a), just as mocking produces suffering for those who reject wisdom. What is evident is that the learner must choose which path to follow, and the choice that is made will lead to predictable ends. In the final analysis, the teacher gives instructions and warnings together with reasons to justify the admonitions, but the learner has the freedom to make the decision, and he bears the major responsibility for the decision that he makes.

By employing reasons with the commands, the teacher is moving away from the stance of the authoritative expert to that of a persuader. The teacher challenges the learner to think through the issue and to obey the command because it is the

mind, God's all-seeing eye is upon him, watching and observing, weighing and judging (see 15:3; Job 31:4; 34:21; Heb. 4:13).'

[15] Nel (1982: 20) notes that Proverbs 9:9 is constructed with an implicit command-with-reason form: 'In both these two admonitions the motivative clauses (*we* + Impf) linguistically seem to be instances of ordinary co-ordination. They are however factual statements about the final consequence of the prescribed behaviour in the admonitions (v. 9aa and 9ba). Here we have one of the shortest forms of an admonition accompanied, evidently, by a motivation.'

wise thing to do. Thus, the teacher is a spiritual director whose role is to counter the natural aimlessness of the learner, for as Eaton (1989: 27) remarks, 'left to themselves, beginners flounder from one extreme to the other. The experienced sage can establish lines by which the disciple can develop the self-control necessary for the good ends in view.'

Command with reasons and illustrations

On some occasions the teacher not only gives reasons to support his commands, but he also augments the logical reasons for obedience with compelling illustrations designed to persuade the learner. The illustrations employ the rhetorical strategy of pathos, for the teacher moves the learner to action by the intentional heightening of emotions (Crenshaw 1981b: 19).

In Proverbs 1:10–19 the teacher presents a hypothetical situation, to support the command to resist the enticements of sinners (1:10). Garrett (1993: 69) notes the significance of this true-to-life illustration in the first passage of instruction in the book:

> Proverbs does not begin its instruction with lofty or abstract analysis but with a simple and straightforward appeal for the reader to reject association with criminals. From the very outset, therefore, this book is grounded in the lives and problems of real people.

The hypothetical situation that is sketched by the teacher uses realistic dialogue to disclose the powerful impulse of peer pressure which confronts the learner. The repeated use of first-person-plural forms reflects the pull of youthful peers against the authority of the teacher.[16] The rhetoric of the illustration captures the desire for self-determination which the young

---

[16] Newsom (1989: 145) analyses well the language of Proverbs 1:11–14: 'The persuaders are not fathers hierarchically related to the son, but peers. Their speech uses the cohortative rather than the direct imperative. Feature pronouns are not the counterposed "I–you" pair but the often repeated "us," "we." The egalitarian subtext is made explicit in verb 14b, "we will all share a common purse." The rival discourse against which the father argues can be made visible in its general outlines: it is one with a horizontal rather than a vertical structure of authority, based not on patriarchal family affiliation but on

learner undoubtedly feels, and which is the point of attack exploited by his peers.

Once the learner has sensed the power of the enticement by imaginatively entering into the hypothetical situation, the teacher repeats the prohibition (1:15), and then gives reasons why the learner should refuse to go along with his peers. This course of action, he says, is both evil (1:16) and foolish (1:17–19). Employing another illustration, of a net spread before birds (1:17),[17] the teacher concludes that those who lie in wait for others will themselves be destroyed (1:18–19). In Yahweh's ordered world evil actions lead to calamity, so the learner should choose to resist the pressures of his peers. The illustrations heighten his awareness of the danger, the command instructs him how to act, and the reasons provide logical rationale to persuade the learner to adopt the wise course of action.

Proverbs 7 is a long passage of instruction that uses illustration with powerful effect. In the attempt to direct the learner to a wholehearted embrace of wisdom, the teacher must also bolster his resistance to the seductions of folly. Recognizing that the learner is a young man for whom sexual temptation is no doubt especially alluring, the teacher employs as a potent, realistic illustration the description of his own observation of a young man seduced by an adulteress. As McKane (1970: 332) remarks, the teacher

> . . . relies on his descriptive powers and his ability to reconstruct imaginatively the woman's stratagems and seductive conversation, so that the warning is conveyed not by schematized instruction, but by introducing the young man into the ways of the world and bringing him to the woman's house, in order to show him that it

---

common enterprise, and one that offers young men immediate access to wealth rather than the deferred wealth of inheritance.'

[17] The difficult metaphor in Proverbs 1:17 is explained well by McKane (1970: 271): 'The bird watches the process of laying the bait, but this has no deterrent effect on it. It will go for the grain just as it would have done if it had not seen it being put down. The bird has been given every reason to exercise prudence and caution; its suspicions should have been awakened, but it is so much the slave of its appetite that it follows a compulsive desire to eat the grain. So it is with the highwaymen who cannot control their appetite for wealth and who are incapable of benefiting from the warnings which would deter reasonable and disciplined men from courses of action which must inevitably destroy them.'

is a death trap and that only a fool will satisfy his desire
at such a price.

The illustration in Proverbs 7:6–23 draws its power through
the literary devices it uses. Though the teacher professes to
describe a specific situation that he has seen, the picture of a
careless youth at night being propositioned by an immoral
woman (7:6–13) is most likely a scene that the learner himself
has witnessed numerous times. Dialogue lends a sense of reality
to the situation as the woman flatters the youth and counters his
anticipated objections (7:14–20). The elaborate description of
the woman's bed (7:16–17), with the erotic overtones in the
terms she selects,[18] enables the learner to feel vicariously the
force of the enticement. Through the rhetorical strategy of
illustration the learner is involved in the emotions of the
imaginative situation, so that he experiences how compelling
the temptation can be. When the teacher drops the picture to
reassert the principle in 7:24–27, his warning is made more
effective because the learner is sensitized by the illustration to
the danger against which the teacher is warning him.

Command with consequences

In this category of instruction, the command is linked with an
indirect motivation. The teacher is not as directive as when
giving logical reasons to support the command. The teacher
desires the same outcome, the learner's obedience, but the
rhetorical form places a higher degree of responsibility in the
hands of the learner. The teacher presents the issues and
explains what consequences can be expected, but then leaves
the decision to the learner.

In Proverbs 1:8–9 the teacher exhorts the learner to listen to
his parents' instruction. He follows this command with a positive
incentive as he states the beneficial consequences that the
obedient learner will enjoy: 'They will be a garland to grace your
head and a chain to adorn your neck' (1:9). The teacher
appeals to the learner's good sense (Aitken 1986: 17), for
obedience to his parents' teaching will confer an honoured
status upon him.

[18] *Cf.* Whybray 1994b: 115.

Proverbs 5:1–6 uses a negative approach, for the command to listen to the teacher's words (5:1–2) is reinforced by a description of the danger which the adulteress poses for the learner (5:3–6).[19] The teacher acknowledges the initial attractiveness of the woman, but he emphasizes that she leads to bitterness and death. The statement of negative consequences itself is the warning for the learner, but he is left to make his own decision.

Proverbs 2 comprises a single complex sentence containing a set of conditions (2:1–4) and the resultant consequences (2:5–22). In place of the usual command, the teacher changes the rhetoric from authoritative direction to recommendation (McKane 1970: 278). This approach enables the teacher to guide the learner through the logical process that will equip him to make wise judgments (Fox 1994: 241).

If the learner accepts wisdom enthusiastically (2:1–4), then he will understand the fear of Yahweh (2:5) and he will have understanding for life (2:9). In addition, wisdom will give protection from both the evil man (2:12–15) and the evil woman (2:16–19). Over the long term of life, wisdom will provide stability, but wickedness will lead to insecurity (2:20–22). By framing the lesson as conditions leading to consequences, the teacher points out the impact of the learner's decision. What is clear is that the learner himself must make that decision, and what he decides will have a profound effect on his life.

Command with rhetorical questions

When a command is followed by rhetorical questions, the teacher pointedly brings the learner to the place of personal decision. In Proverbs 6:20–35 the teacher begins by addressing

[19] McKane (1970: 312) observes: 'The warning against the seductive and alluring woman is a stock one in the international Instruction, and it is improbable that its appearance in the biblical book of Proverbs requires the specialized interpretation which Boström advances. Such an admonition as this has its occasion in universal conditions of human frailty, and what is envisaged here is the same vulnerability of young men to affairs with women as is touched on in the Egyptian Instruction, in the Babylonian *Counsels of Wisdom* and in *Ahikar*. It is a robust man-to-man warning against the consequences of liaisons with loose women. It is not pitched in a key of high-souled moral revulsion or pietism, but is rather a sober, earthy estimate of the disastrous results which flow from this particular manifestation of indiscipline.'

the learner in the second person (6:20–26). He exhorts the youth to listen to his parents' instruction, for their commands are the way to life which provides protection from the immoral woman.

In Proverbs 6:27–28 the teacher changes his form from direct address to third-person rhetorical questions:

> Can a man scoop fire into his lap
>   without his clothes being burned?
> Can a man walk on hot coals
>   without his feet being scorched?[20]

As Crenshaw (1980: 23) notes:

> ... these questions demand a negative answer and function as the equivalent of a strong statement: no one can carry live coals in his garments without setting them on fire, and nobody can walk on glowing coals without burning his feet.

The fact that the rhetorical questions can assume that the learner would answer in keeping with the intent of the teacher indicates that the speaker is quoting a saying that is implicitly an argument from consensus (Crenshaw 1981b: 14) commanding universal assent.

The teacher continues to speak in the third person in Proverbs 6:30–35 as he makes observations of life which support the implicit answer to the rhetorical questions he has posed. Proverbs 6:30 has been variously interpreted by translators and commentators, some construing it as a third rhetorical question, but others rendering it as a statement. The textual evidence for an interrogative particle is scanty (Cohen 1952: 37; Whybray 1994b: 108), so even though a rhetorical question could make

---

[20] Alden (1983: 60) observes that the images employed in the questions suggest illicit sex, in keeping with the message of the passage: 'The images of fire and hot coals are probably used because each implies a second meaning; scooping fire into a man's lap illustrates holding another man's wife, and since elsewhere in Scripture "feet" is a euphemism for the male organ (cf. Isa. 6:2; 7:20; Gen. 49:10; Judg. 3:24; 1 Sam. 24:3; 2 Sam. 11:8), walking on the "hot coals" of illicit sex are [sic] certain to burn or harm one's manhood.'

good sense in the passage (McKane 1970: 330; Aitken 1986: 72), it is better to view 6:30 as a statement.

By reinforcing his command to the learner with rhetorical questions the teacher places the responsibility for the decision squarely in the learner's hands. The rhetorical questions are highly persuasive, because they represent the logical consensus of the society, but what is of primary significance is that the learner must choose whether to act in accord with the obvious answers to the questions, or in conscious rejection of them.

Incentive

Proverbs 3:13–18 and 8:12–21 appeal to the learner by extolling the benefits of wisdom. By describing the intrinsic good of wisdom and the instrumental benefits which it can provide, the teacher endeavours to create in the learner a desire to choose what is best. In these passages there is no explicit command, no logical rationale, and no direct motivation. The teacher simply presents the virtues of wisdom as an incentive for the learner's own choice.

In Proverbs 3:13–18 the teacher abandons the typical commands that predominate in Proverbs 1 – 9. In place of authoritative teaching, he summons the learner to celebration by framing the passage as a beatitude. The opening line, 'Blessed is the man who finds wisdom' (3:13a), is answered by the concluding verse, 'She is a tree of life to those who embrace her; those who lay hold of her will be blessed' (3:18). The body of the passage comprises several statements of the benefits that wisdom gives to those who find her (3:14–17).[21] Clearly, the teacher has not moved away from his goal of challenging the learner to accept the way of wisdom, but the rhetorical strategy he uses is more indirect than are the commands which he employs elsewhere. As McKane (1970: 289) in agreement with Zimmerli notes, the beatitude form is 'halfway between

---

[21] Whybray (1994b: 65) observes: 'This poem is quite different in style from the preceding Instruction. It is a hymn in praise of Wisdom, and is to that extent similar to hymns in praise of various goddesses from the ancient Near East. It differs, however, from the self-praising speeches by Wisdom in 1:20–33 and 8:1–36 in that it is couched in the third person, and in that respect it resembles the poem about Wisdom in Job 28.'

statement and admonition . . . having the character of summons, but lacking direct address.'

The extended call of personified wisdom in Proverbs 8
includes a passage in which wisdom recommends herself
because of the benefits she confers on humans who love her.
Wisdom provides competence for personal living (8:12–14) and
for communal rule (8:15–16). The wealth that wisdom provides
includes both material prosperity and benefits that are better
than fine gold and silver (8:17–21), for it is enduring and
honourable. Wisdom does not issue a command, or even
provide explicit rationale for the desired response by the
learner. Instead, wisdom sets before him the benefits that she
gives to those who embrace her, with the hope that the learner
will appropriate for himself the available blessings by choosing
to love her.

Invitation

Proverbs 9 is a fitting conclusion to the initial section of the
book. The wise teacher juxtaposes two personifications of
wisdom and folly issuing parallel invitations to the learner.[22] In
each picture the person is described: wisdom in 9:1–3, and folly
in 9:13–15. Then the words of invitation are heard: wisdom
inviting the learner to her banquet of life (9:4–6), and folly
enticing the learner to her feast of death (9:16–18). In keeping
with the recurrent portrayal in Proverbs 1 – 9 of the two ways
open to humans, it is appropriate that the final chapter of the
section should use the device of contrast as the teacher builds to
his dramatic and pedagogical climax (Whybray 1994a: 45).

Wisdom speaks in words of invitation, rather than in
commands. Having prepared a lavish banquet (9:2) in her
opulent house (9:1),[23] wisdom summons those who are simple:
'Come, eat my food and drink the wine I have mixed. Leave
your simple ways and you will live; walk in the way of

[22] Blenkinsopp (1991: 466) details how the deliberate strategy of contrasting
the women representing wisdom and folly draws together much of the data of
Proverbs 1 – 9.

[23] Despite the suggestions of some that the seven-pillared house of wisdom
has cultic or cosmological overtones, it seems better to agree with Aitken (1986:
90) and Whybray (1994b: 142–143) that it indicates a patrician mansion
representing security and splendour.

understanding' (9:5–6). Her call is an invitation to the learner to choose the path of wisdom with its attendant benefits.

Using language[24] similar to Proverbs 9:1–6, folly utters her invitation in 9:13–18. The parallel structure, however, only highlights the jarring contrast between the two women and their appeals. Folly is brash (9:13–15) as she seeks to entice the simple to her meretricious hospitality, for she says, 'Stolen water is sweet; food eaten in secret is delicious!' (9:17). If the reference to stolen water can be contrasted with the admonition to 'drink water from your own cistern' (5:15), then folly is tempting the youths with the compelling allurement of prurient sensuality. What she does not say is that those who accept the invitation to be her guests in reality choose death for themselves.

The juxtaposition of these two invitations makes a powerful rhetorical point. Ultimately, it is the learner who must decide between the alternatives. The teacher has a crucial function in bringing the learner to the point where he can recognize the issue and understand the consequences of the alternatives, but only the learner can decide which voice to follow. That is the climactic point of decision to which Proverbs 1 – 9 leads.[25] As O'Conner (1988: 40) summarizes, 'Proverbial wisdom assumes that people are capable of choosing, are free to choose, indeed, must choose their own course of action in life.'

Conclusion

In Proverbs 1 – 9 the teacher employs numerous rhetorical strategies in instructing the learner. In directive modes, such as address and description, the teacher is central to the learning

---

[24] Clifford (1993: 64) remarks: '. . . good prototypes for the temptress exist in ancient literature: Ishtar in Gilgamesh vi.1–79, Anat in the Ugaritic Aqhat legend (KTU 1.17.vi.2–45), and Calypso and Circe in the Odyssey (Odyssey V.202–209, X). In each, a goddess of love offers love or marriage to a young man – Gilgamesh, Aqhat, or Odysseus – which actually threatens death or transformation of his mortal life.'

[25] Yee (1989: 53) states: '. . . the author of Proverbs 1 – 9 arranges the speeches of Lady Wisdom and of the "foreign woman" in a particular macrostructure in which he highlights the virtues and attractions of the former, while exposing the terrible risks of the latter. The author characterizes the two women as competitors for the same man, the son instructed by his father. Both women are described in dangerously similar terms; both speak perilously similar messages to beckon the young man to their respective houses.'

process. The virtual absence of explanation, rationale or illustration implies that the learner is expected to accept the instruction on the basis of the authority of the teacher. Similarly, when a set of conditions precedes a command, the teacher is using a technique that is highly directive as he endeavours to lead the learner into the way of wisdom.

The majority of rhetorical strategies in Proverbs 1 – 9 combine commands by the teacher with some type of substantiation designed to persuade the learner to choose to act in accordance with the teacher's direction. Logical, illustrative, pragmatic and literary devices are used to appeal to the learner. It is evident that these rhetorical forms regard the learner as a direct participant in the learning process, for he is able to choose how he will act. The teacher sets before the learner a persuasive case as he seeks to motivate the learner toward a wise decision, but the responsibility for the decision belongs primarily to the learner.

This focus on learner involvement is even more pronounced in the passages in Proverbs 1 – 9 that speak in terms of incentive and invitation. When using these rhetorical strategies, the teacher is very much in the background of the instructional process. With scarcely a hint of direct exhortation, the teacher extols the potential blessings of wisdom and pictures the temptation by folly. It is the learner, however, who must choose how to respond to the alternatives presented to him.

Chapter Six

Role of the teacher

In every pedagogical situation there is a relationship between the teacher and the learner. In formal educational structures, this relationship is stated in explicit terms, with clearly defined roles for both parties. In informal contexts, the roles often are not spelled out in specific language, but there is an implicit relationship between teacher and learner that governs their interactions with each other.

In Proverbs 1 – 9, what role or roles does the teacher play, and what is the nature of his responsibility in the educational endeavour? The teacher's role is not stated in definitive terms in Proverbs 1 – 9. Nevertheless, the rhetorical strategies that the teacher uses provide a wealth of implications that indicate how his role is envisioned in this text of biblical wisdom. On the one hand, instances of highly directive rhetoric suggest that the teacher plays the role of the expert authority. This view of the teacher's role would correspond well with traditional pedagogical theory. On the other hand, examples of non-directive rhetoric imply that the teacher functions as a facilitator who encourages the learner's independent competence, which is the teacher's primary role in progressive pedagogical theory.

To do justice to all of the evidence that has been presented in chapter 5, the role of the teacher must account for the full range of rhetoric observable in Proverbs 1 – 9. This chapter will examine both the highly directive utterances and the non-directive utterances of the teacher to determine what they contribute to the question of his role. Then, the more comprehensive metaphor of the guide will be developed as an appropriate description of the multi-faceted role of the teacher.

The teacher as an expert authority

As discussed in chapter 5, several of the rhetorical categories represented in Proverbs 1 – 9 depict the teacher as an expert authority. In the passages in which address is prominent, the teacher speaks with the authoritative voice of a qualified expert. He initiates the pedagogical situation by going to where the learners are and calling for their attention (1:20–21; 8:1–3). In 1:24–31 the teacher pronounces threats if the learner does not listen and obey, but aside from this there is no reference to active learner involvement in the process of learning.

When the teacher uses descriptions, he delivers lectures without significant explanation. The teacher, however, is not claiming for himself power by virtue of his position over the learner. Instead, he is qualified to speak with authority because of his status as a knowledgeable and reliable transmitter of tradition. As Lang (1986: 37) notes, the teacher possesses *auctoritas*, a recognized position of authority validated by the tradition that he teaches:

> The wisdom communicated by teachers does not originate in them nor is it a product of their brilliance. It is the tradition, and nothing else, that is being passed from teacher to student. The teacher's individuality, therefore, does not really matter, even though the teacher speaks emphatically in the first person. The voice of the teacher is the voice of tradition and thus, in a sense, beyond individuality.

The teacher's primary credential for authority is the expert knowledge that he possesses. Speaking in general terms of the authority that teachers in every culture possess, Cleife (1976: 129) observes:

> It is these people who know, who will be placed in positions of authority. By the nature of their expertise and ability they will teach as well as judge and in more civilised societies forms of assessment are employed to establish the possession of such competencies.

The teacher in Proverbs 1 – 9 can speak with authority, because his superior knowledge of wisdom establishes his reliability. He does not claim authority on the basis of his position, but his authority is derived from his expert knowledge of the tradition which he transmits to the learner.

Many of the rhetorical forms employed in Proverbs 1 – 9 use commands. When a command follows a condition, it comprises a highly directive strategy reflecting the authoritative stance of the teacher. More frequently the commands are followed by reasons, consequences, illustrations and other devices designed to elicit a response by the learner. In these cases the teacher is indeed placing a measure of responsibility in the hands of the learner, but the strong didactic tone of the imperatives is undeniable. Although the teacher wants the learner to choose to obey his instructions, he uses forms of rhetoric that make the instructions as compelling as possible.

By speaking as an expert authority, the teacher endeavours to speed up the learning process and to prevent unnecessary, and perhaps painful, detours by the learner. Despite all of its benefits, self-directed learning can be inefficient at best, and it is often dangerous for the uninitiated student. As a knowledge-able and reliable authority, the teacher is in the position to make learning more efficient and less risky for those who are novices.

On the other hand, the role of the teacher as an expert authority implies relative passivity by the learner. Exclusive commitment to this model of teaching could produce mere compliance to indoctrination without genuine personal appro-priation by the learner. It is important, therefore, to balance this aspect of the teacher's role with the rest of the evidence in Proverbs 1 – 9, which suggests a more significant degree of involvement by the learner. It is true that Proverbs 1 – 9 does portray the teacher as an expert who actively directs the learning process, but that is not the exclusive or even predominant depiction of the role of the teacher in this text.

The teacher as a facilitator

The passages in Proverbs 1 – 9 in which the teacher uses the rhetorical strategies of incentive and invitation suggest that the role of the teacher is more of a facilitator than a director. When incentive is prominent (3:13–18; 8:12–21), the teacher does not use explicit commands or direct motivations. Instead, he presents the advantages of the way of wisdom, but leaves the choice up to the learner. The learner is given knowledge and is influenced toward the desirable decision by the language of the teacher, but the indirect mode of instruction implies that the learner bears primary responsibility for the alternative he chooses and the consequences which that decision entails.

In the culminating pair of invitations in Proverbs 9:1–6, 13–18, the teacher recedes into the background as the woman of wisdom and the woman of folly appeal directly to the learner. Aside from the introductory descriptions of the two speakers and the teacher's caution against the allurement of folly in 9:18 ('But little do they know that the dead are there, that her guests are in the depths of the grave'), the learner hears personally the two alternatives. The teacher is not mediating between the learner and the rival invitations. Instead, the teacher's role is to bring the learner to the point where he himself is capable of evaluating the alternatives and making a responsible decision. The teacher equips the learner to make the decision, but his role is not to decide for the learner what he must do.

In recent pedagogical theory the role of the teacher as a facilitator has become the dominant model for education in North America. For example, Combs (1982: 166) remarks:

> Increasingly, teaching is understood, not as a matter of control and direction, but of help and facilitation. Teachers are asked to be facilitators rather than controllers, helpers rather than directors. They are asked to be assisters, encouragers, enrichers, inspirers. The concept of teachers as makers, forcers, molders, or coercers is no longer regarded as the ideal role for teachers and the position is firmly buttressed by evidence from research. Modern thinking about teaching regards it as a process of ministering to student growth rather than a process of control and management of behaviour.

When the teacher is viewed as a facilitator, the learners are active participants in the learning process, not passive recipients of instruction provided by the teacher. Consequently, 'teachers are responsible primarily for providing constructive feedback, for encouraging students to think beyond the obvious, and for providing the guidelines and parameters within which problem-solving can take place' (Heck and Williams 1984: 75).[1] The facilitator does not direct learning so much as assist the learner to learn for himself. By creating conditions conducive to the learner's growth, the teacher helps the learner, but with minimal direction. According to this perspective, 'Good teachers are not makers and molders. They are skillful helpers, aids, assistants or facilitators, ministers to the organism's own basic need. Teaching is a helping profession' (Combs 1982: 74).

The model of the teacher as a facilitator corresponds well with the relativistic epistemology and axiology of postmodernism. As Johnson (1995: 155–171) discusses, postmodernism has become the methodological premise upon which much of contemporary educational theory and practice is based. Instead of the teacher directing the students toward truth and moral judgments, in the current climate of most universities and schools the teacher encourages the students 'to reason their way to a personal moral philosophy after a critical consideration of alternatives' (1995: 163). When the role of the teacher is defined as a facilitator, then the learner is central to the pedagogical task. The teacher is more non-directive, granting a high degree of freedom to the learner.

Although the rhetorical forms of incentive and invitation in Proverbs 1 – 9 do coincide in large measure with the model of the teacher as a facilitator, this evidence must be viewed within the larger framework of the section as a whole. In that context, the role of the teacher does include facilitation of the learning process, but it is simply not accurate to claim that this text in the wisdom corpus presents the teacher as having little authority over the learner.[2]

[1] Hyman (1970: 44) develops a similar concept of the role of the teacher as an enabler of the learner: 'The teacher, as enabler, challenges the student to find things out for himself. He leads the student to generalizations and inferences regarding the subject matter under study. The teacher prompts the student. He, in effect, says to the student, "If you wish to know, you must work with the data from experience itself. Through your own inquiry will come knowledge."'

[2] In light of the evidence in Proverbs 1 – 9, Brueggemann (1972: 87) is inaccurate in his depiction of the teacher in Old Testament wisdom: 'The mood and method of the wisdom teacher was simply to make observations on the actions and choices which for that situation moved things toward "life." Such actions and choices might be generalized, for they surely also applied to

When the facilitation model is emphasized too prominently, then the teacher's legitimate responsibility in the pedagogical task is undervalued. In light of the total data of Proverbs 1 – 9, it is better to say that the teacher is a vital component, though not the single determinative factor, affecting the learning process. In this text the role of the teacher includes an element of facilitation, but the preponderance of the evidence demands a more comprehensive model.

The teacher as a guide

As has been demonstrated, the rhetoric of Proverbs 1 – 9 intimates elements of both the expert and the facilitator models of the teacher. Neither the expert model nor the facilitator model alone, however, does justice to all of the data. To account for the full range of the information relative to the role of the teacher in Proverbs 1 – 9, a more general metaphor is necessary. The metaphor of the teacher as a guide includes both direction by the teacher and the active involvement of the student in the learning process. As a guide, the teacher has experience in life. The teacher communicates this superior understanding to the learner, but at the same time the learner is given freedom to investigate life and to make decisions. The teacher provides a framework within which the learner can independently evaluate life's decisions.

This concept of the teacher as guide corresponds well with the approach taken by several pedagogical theorists. For example, although John Dewey is best known for his emphasis upon the learner, even he at times views the teacher as a guide. He states:

> Guiding is not external imposition. It is freeing the life-process for its own most adequate fulfilment . . . There are those who see no alternative between forcing the child from without, or leaving him entirely alone. Seeing no alternative, some choose one mode, some another. Both fall into the same fundamental error. Both fail to see that development is a definite process,

---

other situations as well, but there is characteristically no insistence that they have enduring worth or ultimate authority.'

having its own law which can be fulfilled only when adequate and normal conditions are provided (1943: 17).

Others employ closely related metaphors which also encompass both the teacher's direction and the learner's active involvement. For example, Heck and Williams (1984: 60) envision the teacher as a navigator:

> The ideal learning environment is one in which students work *with* rather than depend upon the teacher – an environment in which the pupil assumes the basic responsibility for learning but uses the teacher as a guide, a consultant, a resource person, and many times as a 'navigator' for the learning effort.

Combs (1982: 111) views the teacher's role as a helper-catalyst, who helps the learners to achieve maximum personal growth while they remain in her field of influence. Ober *et al.* (1971: 142) see the teacher as a coach, who assesses the situation and the student, and then 'selects the strategy that, in his professional judgment, will best suit the given situation.'

In Proverbs 1 – 9 the goal of the wise teacher is to guide the learner to live within Yahweh's world. The focus is upon the development of the inner person, not just upon compliance with a pattern of external actions. The teacher endeavours to bring the learner to personal maturity, for as Rylaarsdam (1964: 29) concludes:

> Wisdom is the knowledge and experience about life and living taught and explained by the sages; it is a pupil's capacity for mature and right understanding and judgment, a capacity which results when he fully comprehends and chooses as his own what he is taught . . .

When teaching is viewed as guidance of the learner to independent maturity, then the role of the teacher changes over time. Since the learner begins as a novice, the teacher at first must take on the role of the expert in providing a high degree of direction. At the initial stages of learning, the teacher exerts maximum guidance in order to speed up the learning process and to minimize mistakes that will have to be corrected later. As the learner grows in maturity, however, the teacher can become a less directive facilitator, allowing the learner to use the developing skills necessary for independent life.

The terms 'guide' and 'guidance' are used only three times in the NIV translation of Proverbs 1 – 9. The preface in Proverbs 1:5 includes among the goals of education this exhortation: '. . . let the wise listen and add to their learning, and let the discerning get guidance [*taḥbulôt*].' This term speaks of expertise in navigation, or the art of piloting through the confusion of life (see page 71). The wise teacher says to the learner, 'I guide [*hōrêtîkā*] you in the way of wisdom and lead you along straight paths' (4:11). This verb, the Hiphil form of *yārâ*, is also found in 4:4, 5:13 and 6:13. Speaking of the parental instructions, Proverbs 6:22 promises, 'When you walk, they will guide [*tanḥeh*] you; when you sleep, they will watch over you; when you awake, they will speak to you.'

Although there is a paucity of explicit references to guidance in Proverbs 1 – 9, the rhetorical strategies employed by the teacher and analysed in chapter 5 of this study strongly suggest the metaphor of the teacher as guide. When the teacher uses commands supported by reasons (*e.g.* 4:10–19), he directs the learner toward right thinking. The teacher guides the learner toward reasonable action through persuasion, not through coercion.

In passages such as Proverbs 7, in which the teacher supports his commands by illustrations, the learner enters imaginatively into the situation set forth by the teacher. The teacher guides the learner down the path to decision by walking him through a realistic scenario. The learner must choose whether or not to obey the direction which the teacher has communicated through principle and picture.

When commands are reinforced by consequences, as in Proverbs 2, greater responsibility is placed in the hands of the learner. The alternatives with their consequences are spelled out for the learner, but the teacher leaves the decision up to him. Similarly, when commands are followed by rhetorical questions (6:20–35), the learner must choose whether or not to act according to the logical answers to the questions. The teacher presents a reasonable case by which he endeavours to guide the learner toward wisdom, but the ultimate choice is placed in the learner's hands.

In addition to the frequent use of commands coupled with various strategies designed to encourage the learner's personal decision, there are hints of the role of the teacher as a guide throughout all of Proverbs 1 – 9. Even the passages in which the teacher is viewed as an expert authority contain elements, however slight, of learner involvement (see pages 126–127). Moreover, as Proverbs 9:18 demonstrates, the rhetoric most compatible with the notion of the teacher as a facilitator also includes direction by the teacher.

In order for learners to be able to make rational and wise decisions, they need an intellectual and moral framework for their choices. Before they can exercise independent competence in a responsible and constructive way, learners must be guided into patterns of discipline. Eaton (1989: 27) observes that 'left to themselves, beginners flounder from one extreme to the other. The experienced sage can establish lines by which the disciple can develop the self-control necessary for the good ends in view.' In fact the teacher has the obligation to use his greater experience and insight as he guides the learner into the right paths.[3] The role of the teacher in Proverbs 1 – 9, then, is best described as that of a guide, who uses his expertise in knowledge and authoritative position to lead the learner to the point of independent competence in living wisely in Yahweh's world.

Conclusion

Although the teacher is viewed in Proverbs 1 – 9 as both an expert authority and a facilitator in various passages, neither of these models is sufficiently broad to account for all of the relevant data. Texts that focus on the teacher as an expert represent him as a reliable transmitter of tradition who is qualified to speak with authority. By his expert knowledge the

[3] Dewey (1938: 31–32) argues trenchantly: 'The greater maturity of experience which should belong to the adult as educator puts him in a position to evaluate each experience of the young in a way in which the one having the less mature experience cannot do. It is then the business of the educator to see in what direction an experience is heading. There is no point in his being more mature if, instead of using his greater insight to help organize the conditions of the experience of the immature, he throws away his insight.'

teacher can accelerate the learning process and prevent unnecessary risk for the learner. On the other hand, the learner becomes a relatively passive recipient of knowledge, rather than an active participant in the learning process.

When the teacher uses incentive and invitation as his rhetorical devices, he plays the role of the facilitator. In this role the teacher does not direct the learner, but instead creates conditions that are conducive to the learner's independent growth. In Proverbs 1 – 9 facilitation is not elevated above direction, but it is integrally connected with it. The teacher is always viewed as a vital active component in the learning process, even when the responsibility of the learner is most in the foreground.

The metaphor of the guide best pictures the multi-faceted role of the teacher in Proverbs 1 – 9. As a guide, the teacher uses his knowledge and experience to provide direction for the learner. The ultimate goal, however, is that the learner will develop independent competence in living responsibly in Yahweh's world. The teacher's progression from expert authority to facilitator parallels the intellectual and moral development of the learner. When the learner is a novice, the teacher must exert a higher degree of direction, but as the learner grows in wisdom, the teacher is able to become more of an enabler to assist the learner as he makes his own decisions. Thus, the teacher's role is to be a guide, to motivate the learners on to maturity. The teacher is at times an expert, at times a facilitator, but always the guide, pointing the learners toward their own independent competence.

Chapter Seven

Role of the learner

In order for learning to take place, both the teacher and the learner must fulfil their proper roles. The previous chapter delineated the role of the teacher in Proverbs 1 – 9 as that of a guide who uses his knowledge and experience to lead the learner into independent competence for living in Yahweh's world. This chapter analyses the role of the learner. Granted that the teacher is a guide, what role does the learner play in the accomplishment of a successful educational experience?

Prior discussions of the rhetorical strategies used in instruction (chapter 5) and of the role of the teacher (chapter 6) provide implications for the role of the learner. For example, when highly directive language is used, the teacher is portrayed as an expert authority whom the learner must obey. On the other hand, when the teacher uses the rhetoric of invitation, the learner bears the responsibility for choosing whether or not to accept the offer that has been extended.

Proverbs 1 – 9 contains additional data that help to define the role of the learner. The explicit actions and attitudes which the teacher enjoins upon the learner provide testimony to the responsibility borne by the learner. Taken together, these references correlate well with the major categories in the affective domain of the taxonomy of educational objectives developed in the seminal study of Krathwohl (1964). In this chapter the data in Proverbs 1 – 9 relative to the role of the learner will be discussed in terms of the categories of Krathwohl as summarized by Gronlund (1985). The prominent aspects of the role of the learner are receiving, responding, valuing and assimilating. Through these attitudes and activities, the learner develops a comprehensive and coherent philosophy of life. In the context of Proverbs 1 – 9 the role of the learner is to internalize the values of wisdom as communicated through the guidance of the teacher.

The learner must receive wisdom

At its most basic level, learning requires a willingness to attend to particular phenomena or stimuli (Gronlund 1985: 38). The role of the learner, then, begins with selective attention by the learner. The learner must be disposed to listen to instruction, which implies a measure of tacit recognition of the authority of the teacher. Consequently, the learner from the start must be sufficiently humble to be willing to learn from others. O'Conner (1988: 41–42) observes:

> To become wise individuals must have open minds; they must be able to stand before life and to learn from it. Some people are incapable of learning, not because they lack intelligence but because they lack humility. Moreover, such people disrupt the community because they are unable to learn from others . . . The humble, on the other hand, are those who are aware that there is more to life than their limited experience of it. They can recognize the narrowness of their own frame of reference, and so they are teachable. Conversely, people without humility join the ranks of the fools and suffer the consequences.

To learn wisdom, one must be willing to listen to those who are wise.

The notion of the learner as a receiver in Proverbs 1 – 9 is communicated by several verbs, which are most frequently used in exhortations by the teacher to the learner. The verb *lāqaḥ* is employed four times as the teacher charges the learner to receive instruction:

> . . . for acquiring [*lāqaḥat*] a disciplined and prudent life,
> doing what is right and just and fair . . . (1:3).

> My son, if you accept [*tiqqaḥ*] my words
> and store up my commands within you . . . (2:1).

> Listen, my son, accept [*wᵉqaḥ*] what I say,
> and the years of your life will be many (4:10).

Choose [$q^e\hbar\hat{u}$] my instruction instead of silver,
knowledge rather than choice gold . . . (8:10).

In addition to the verbal forms of *lāqah*, the cognate noun *leqah*
appears three times:

. . . let the wise listen and add to their learning [*leqah*],
and let the discerning get guidance (1:5).

I give you sound learning [*leqah*],
so do not forsake my teaching (4:2).

Instruct a wise man and he will be wiser still;
teach a righteous man and he will add to his learning
[*leqah*] (9:9).

Oesterley (1929: 4) notes that *leqah* embodies the Jewish concept
of education as the transmission of tradition from the teacher to
the learner. He says:

> The word for 'learning' (*lekach*) here used is compara-
> tively rare, but well illustrates the Jewish method of
> acquiring knowledge; it comes from the root meaning
> 'to take', or 'receive', referring to that which is
> received by being handed down . . . In Rabbinical
> literature it is used in the sense of a 'lesson' delivered
> by the teacher to his pupil; the highest praise which
> one Rabbi can utter of another is contained in the
> Mishna tractate *Pirqê 'Abôth* ii.11, where it is said:
> 'Eliezer ben Hyrcanos is a cistern (plastered) with
> lime which loseth not a drop;' *i.e.* everything which he
> had received from his teachers he retained; the further
> implication being that he was therefore in a position to
> hand it down to others.

The *lqh* word group suggests a willingness to assimilate past
tradition. Instead of demanding the right to his own originality,
the learner must appropriate 'that wisdom which is the deposit
of the best minds of many generations' (McKane 1970: 266). In
order that his personal judgments may have a solid basis, the
learner must first achieve expertise in received wisdom, which

precedes effectiveness in life (Cox 1982b: 100).

The teacher uses forms of *qāšab* on four occasions, three times in juxtaposition with the verb *nāṭâ*, as he challenges the learner to heed his words:

> . . . turning [*haqšîb*] your ear to wisdom
> and applying [*taṭṭeh*] your heart to understanding (2:2).

> My son, pay attention [*haqšîbâ*] to what I say;
> listen [*haṭ*] closely to my words (4:20).

> My son, pay attention [*haqšîbâ*] to my wisdom,
> listen [*haṭ*] well to my words of insight . . . (5:1).

> Now then, my sons, listen to me;
> pay attention [*haqšîbû*] to what I say (7:24).

In this closely related set of verbs, *qāšab* usually communicates the literal reality of attentiveness, with *nāṭâ* representing the same concept through the metaphor of turning or inclining the ear or the heart toward the teacher. As the conditional structure of Proverbs 2 indicates, receptivity to wisdom (the protases in 2:1–4) must precede the rewards of wisdom (the apodoses in 2:5–22).[1] The learner must begin with an attentive spirit, not an argumentative or autonomous spirit. McKane (1970: 282) notes well:

> . . . it is not originality nor argumentativeness nor critical independence in the face of instruction that is demanded of the pupil. He must indeed be attentive and keen (v. 2), like one who cries out for insight and shouts for discernment, but the authority of the teacher must not be called into question.

Those who close their minds to the wise teacher will find that

---

[1] Garrett (1993:74) remarks: 'This whole text hinges on an enormous "if" clause (vv. 1–4). The "if" represents a decision that every young man must make. He can either go in the way of Wisdom and find life, true love, and most importantly God, or he can turn his back on her and find only bitterness, isolation, and death. He cannot opt out of making this decision or choose a little of one and a little of the other.'

they have closed the door to wisdom for themselves (Aitken 1986: 27).

The verb used most frequently in Proverbs 1 – 9 to speak of the learner as a receiver is *šāmaʻ*. This term, found in a variety of verbal forms, occurs in a positive sense eleven times:

> . . . let the wise listen [*yišmaʻ*] and add to their learning,
>   and let the discerning get guidance (1:5).

> Listen [*šᵉʻmaʻ*], my son, to your father's instruction
>   and do not forsake your mother's teaching (1:8).

> . . . but whoever listens [*šōmēaʻ*] to me will live in safety
>   and be at ease, without fear of harm (1:33).

> Listen [*šimʻû*], my sons, to a father's instruction;
>   pay attention and gain understanding (4:1).

> Listen [*šᵉʻmaʻ*], my son, accept what I say,
>   and the years of your life will be many (4:10).

> Now then, my sons, listen [*šimʻû*] to me;
>   do not turn aside from what I say (5:7).

> Now then, my sons, listen [*šimʻû*] to me;
>   pay attention to what I say (7:24).

> Listen [*šimʻû*], for I have worthy things to say;
>   I open my lips to speak what is right (8:6).

> Now then, my sons, listen [*šimʻû*] to me;
>   blessed are those who keep my ways.
> Listen [*šimʻû*] to my instruction and be wise;
>   do not ignore it.
> Blessed is the man who listens [*šōmēaʻ*] to me,
>   watching daily at my doors,
>   waiting at my doorway (8:32–34).

The central feature of this word group is the unquestioning obedience to authority that it enjoins. Whether the authority is the learner's parents (1:8), personified wisdom (1:33; 8:6, 32–

34), or the teacher of wisdom (4:1, 10; 5:7; 7:24), the learner is exhorted to hear and heed the words of instruction.

Proverbs 1 – 9 also defines receptivity from a negative perspective by contrasting it with the lack of attentiveness to the teacher. In 3:1 the learner is warned against neglecting instruction by forgetting the teaching which is available to him. This lack of attentiveness can lead the learner into intentional disobedience, either to his teachers (5:13) or to wisdom in general (1:24–25), a stance which will eventuate in painful consequences (1:26–32). Ultimately, the refusal to receive instruction can produce outright resentment even for the discipline that Yahweh designs for the benefit of the children whom he loves (3:11–12).

The learner must respond to wisdom

The role of the learner involves more than just hearing instruction. In addition to attending to the teacher, the learner must also respond to what has been taught. As a responder, the learner is an active participant in the learning process, not simply a passive observer (Gronlund 1985: 38).

In Proverbs 1 – 9 the role of the learner as a responder is communicated through both positive and negative commands. The teacher charges, 'My son, preserve sound judgment and discernment, do not let them out of your sight . . .' (3:21). For instruction to be effective, the learner must exert effort to retain what wisdom has taught. As McKane (1970: 298) observes, 'constant attention must be given to competence and resourcefulness, and no detail bearing on them is ever to be overlooked or neglected.' The learner's active involvement is an essential component of the educative process.

In Proverbs 6:1–5 a threefold condition is followed by a consequence. The condition in 6:1–2 is designed by the teacher to guide the learner into recognizing the potential problem of imprudent financial commitments:

> My son, if you have put up security for your neighbour,
>   if you have struck hands in pledge for another,
> if you have been trapped by what you said,
>   ensnared by the words of your mouth . . .

The consequence in 6:3–5 exhorts the learner to respond to the problem with active steps:

> . . . then do this, my son, to free yourself,
>   since you have fallen into your neighbour's hands:
> Go and humble yourself;
>   press your plea with your neighbour!
> Allow no sleep to your eyes,
>   no slumber to your eyelids.
> Free yourself, like a gazelle from the hand of the hunter,
>   like a bird from the snare of the fowler.

In responding to the situation, the learner needs to humble himself, accept personal responsibility, and exert every effort to extricate himself from the predicament which he has created unwittingly. It is the learner who must take action in response to the instruction of the teacher.

In Proverbs 6:20–21 the teacher urges the learner to bind upon his heart the instruction from his parents:

> My son, keep your father's commands
>   and do not forsake your mother's teaching.
> Bind them upon your heart for ever;
>   fasten them around your neck.

Aitken (1986: 69) notes the realistic quality of this reminder:

> There is always a temptation for young people to think
> they have outgrown the home truths they were taught
> as children, when they come of age. But their parents'
> teaching, says the sage, if taken to heart and kept in
> clear view, will prove a reliable guide, a watchful guard,
> and an agreeable companion (vv. 21–22).

More than mere attention to instruction is in view here. The learner must accept the instruction as his continual possession. He must both hear and heed what he is taught. He must respond to what he has received.

Proverbs 7:1–3 uses a string of imperatives to challenge the learner to active response to the teacher's words:

My son, keep my words
and store up my commands within you.
Keep my commands and you will live;
guard my teachings as the apple of your eye.
Bind them on your fingers;[2]
write them on the tablet of your heart.

This call to unbroken concentration on wisdom evidences that the learner must do more than listen to instruction which remains external to him. Rather, the learner must grasp the teaching and make it part of the fabric of his life. In other words, the learner takes wisdom to heart and turns it into habits (Kidner 1964: 75). For learning to be effective, the learner must participate actively by personally responding to instruction.

The need for the learner's response is also implied by several negative commands in Proverbs 1 – 9. For example, the teacher warns, 'My son, if sinners entice you, do not give in to them' (1:10), and '. . . my son, do not go along with them, do not set foot on their paths . . .' (1:15). It is true that temptation cannot always be avoided, but it must never be accepted. The learner must neither give in to sinners nor go along with them in their sinful ways.

The teacher says in Proverbs 3:27–28 that merely knowing the right thing to do is not sufficient. Knowledge must be transformed into action.

Do not withhold good from those who deserve it,[3]
when it is in your power to act.
Do not say to your neighbour,
"Come back later; I'll give it tomorrow"[4] –
when you now have it with you.

[2] Whybray (1994b: 111) notes: 'The fingers are obviously a place where one might wear a ring or possibly a protective amulet. But, like the neck (1:9; 3:3, 22; 6:21) they are a part of the body where ornaments would be constantly seen and so could be a reminder of something: they would not "depart from the eyes" (4:21). This is thus another figure expressing the importance of never forgetting the teacher's counsels.'

[3] Aitken (1986:50) remarks well: 'Probably the sage intends his words to be general in scope and applicable in different kinds of circumstances where a neighbour needs our help, but laying the emphasis on his *right* to it rather than his need of it.'

[4] Cohen (1952: 19) elucidates the significance of this line: 'The Rabbis saw in the words a reference to the duty of paying a hired labourer his wage at the end of the day's work (Deut. xxiv. 14f.). It may be more generally applied to one

This instruction counters the selfish spirit that prompts one to defer help to those in need, even though the resources for assistance are available. In reality this is a sin of omission, for there is no response that puts into action what one knows is right.

Throughout Proverbs 1 – 9 the teacher describes the dangers of the way of wickedness or folly. In Proverbs 4:14–15 he cautions the learner to avoid this perilous path:

> Do not set foot on the path of the wicked
> or walk in the way of evil men.
> Avoid it, do not travel on it;
> turn from it and go on your way.

The teacher can describe the peril, but only the learner can decide his path. The teacher is responsible for guiding the learner toward a wise decision, but the learner himself must respond in accordance with what he has been taught if he is to find the path of wisdom and stay on it.

In Proverbs 5:7–8 the teacher uses the powerful image of the adulteress as he elicits response from the learners:

> Now then, my sons, listen to me;
> do not turn aside from what I say.
> Keep to a path far from her,
> do not go near the door of her house . . .

Because the adulteress is so alluring she poses great danger to the young men who are the learners in this context. Knowing this risk, the learners must flee the adulteress, not flirt with her. Being aware of the threat is not sufficient in itself; the learners must actively resist the threat, by living in the light of what they have learned. As learners, they are obliged to respond to the instruction they have received.

The learner must value wisdom

In addition to receiving wisdom and responding to it with obedience, the learner must also value wisdom. By valuing it, the

---

who seeks help; it must not be deferred since it adds to his worries and also increases his sense of shame when he has to repeat his request.'

learner attaches worth to the instruction he has been given, demonstrating a positive appreciation for it. Consequently, the learner's behaviour reflects 'the internalization of a set of specified values' (Gronlund 1985: 38), which in the case of Proverbs 1 – 9 are the values of wisdom (*cf.* chapter 2). Instead of being committed to selfish personal desires, the learner must regard Yahweh's discipline and instruction as the pre-eminent value in life (Eaton 1989: 136).

In Proverbs 2:3–4 the teacher uses four verbs of increasing intensity to communicate that the learner must love wisdom enough to search diligently for it:

> . . . and if you call out for insight
>> and cry aloud for understanding,
> and if you look for it as for silver
>> and search for it as for hidden treasure . . .

Wisdom, he says, is available, but the learner must exert himself to find it.

When the teacher commands, 'Trust in the LORD with all your heart' (Proverbs 3:5a), he urges wholehearted confidence in Yahweh. By concentrating the whole inner life on Yahweh, and finding his sense of security in him, rather than in human resources, the learner places his absolute dependence in the Lord (Aitken 1986: 38).

In Proverbs 3:18 the teacher uses the language of physical intimacy, which would have been particularly poignant to the young men envisioned as the original recipients of the instruction, to encourage the learner to value wisdom. He says of wisdom, 'She is a tree of life to those who embrace her; those who lay hold of her will be blessed.' To receive the blessings wisdom promises, the learner must love wisdom and cleave to it.

The verb *tāmak*, translated 'lay hold of' in 3:18, also introduces the words of the teacher in Proverbs 4:4–8. This passage in many respects is an expansion of the former verse, as the teacher recalls how he himself was instructed in his youth:

> Lay hold of my words with all your heart;
>> keep my commands and you will live.
> Get wisdom, get understanding;
>> do not forget my words or swerve from them.

Do not forsake wisdom, and she will protect you;
    love her, and she will watch over you.
Wisdom is supreme; therefore get wisdom.
    Though it cost all you have, get understanding.
Esteem her, and she will exalt you,
    embrace her, and she will honour you.

Each of the imperatives in this passage stresses the need to value wisdom. The learner must love wisdom (4:6).[5] Four times the learner is charged to get wisdom and understanding (4:5, 7), with the final climactic exhortation, 'Though it cost all you have, get understanding' (4:7b). Furthermore, he must esteem and embrace her (4:8). McKane (1970: 305) remarks:

> Wisdom is an unquestionable first in any order of priorities. She should determine the structure of a man's life, giving it form and proportion and establishing a scale of priorities and a right distribution of emphasis. In return for the protection which she bestows, Wisdom requires of her devotees constancy of allegiance and affection. She must be followed steadfastly and loved without fickleness.

Consequently, the learner is encouraged, 'Hold on to instruction, do not let it go; guard it well, for it is your life' (4:13).

Proverbs 7, which includes the most extensive passage in Proverbs 1 – 9 warning against the danger of the adulteress, begins with a challenge to the learner to give wholehearted devotion to wisdom. The language used in 7:4a, 'Say to wisdom, "You are my sister," ' is reminiscent of the intimate appellations found in Song of Songs 4:9–10. In the context of Proverbs 7, love for wisdom protects the learner from lust for folly. Moreover, this love for wisdom will be amply reciprocated, as the words of personified wisdom in 8:17–21 attest:

---

[5] Whybray (1994b: 77) observes that 'to "love wisdom" does not necessarily mean more than to apply oneself wholeheartedly to its acquisition (12:1; 29:3). But here the context shows that the phrase is used, metaphorically, of the love of a person. In 8:17 personified Wisdom speaks of a *reciprocal* love between herself and those who seek her out.'

I love those who love me,
  and those who seek me find me.
With me are riches and honour,
  enduring wealth and prosperity.
My fruit is better than fine gold;
  what I yield surpasses choice silver.
I walk in the way of righteousness,
  along the paths of justice,
bestowing wealth on those who love me
  and making their treasuries full.

Wisdom, then, should be chosen above all material riches (8:10–11), because there is nothing that can compare with it. Only wisdom is worthy of the learner's love and commitment.

The teacher also uses negative statements and commands to reinforce the point that the learner must value wisdom. Personified wisdom says that fools will suffer destruction because 'they would not accept my advice and spurned my rebuke' (1:30). Their failure to appreciate what wisdom says results in personal calamity.

In Proverbs 3:5b the command to trust Yahweh whole-heartedly is paired with the admonition 'lean not on your own understanding'. As Greenstone (1950: 27) observes, 'Understanding is important and one should make every effort to attain it, but one should not rely on it entirely, since experience has shown that it is fallible and has to have divine support.' The similar warning in 3:7 contrasts confidence in one's personal perceptions with reverence for Yahweh: 'Do not be wise in your own eyes; fear the LORD and shun evil.' The learner must not trust his own perceived wisdom, which is subject to error, but his behaviour must evidence that he values the way of Yahweh. Instead of holding to his own preferences, the learner must 'abdicate his own autonomy in defining his moral code' (Zornberg 1982: 32).

It is clear from Proverbs 1 – 9 that what one loves determines how one lives. In warning the learner against the immoral woman, the teacher cautions, 'Do not lust in your heart after her beauty or let her captivate you with her eyes' (6:25), and 'Do not let your heart turn to her ways or stray into her paths' (7:25). Lust arises from a heart turned in the wrong direction. For the learner to prosper, his heart must be directed toward wisdom.

He must listen to wise instruction, live in accordance with it, and love it wholeheartedly so as to internalize its values.

The learner must assimilate wisdom

The capstone of the role of the learner in Proverbs 1 – 9 is the assimilation of wisdom as a coherent philosophy of life. As the learner develops a pattern of life organized around wisdom he achieves an internally consistent value system (Gronlund 1985: 38). All aspects of life are united by wisdom to form an integrated person living skilfully in Yahweh's ordered world.

This thorough commitment to Yahweh's values is described in the metaphors of Proverbs 3:3:

> Let love and faithfulness never leave you;
>> bind them around your neck,[6]
> write them on the tablet of your heart.

The learner must keep constantly in mind the values which wisdom endeavours to inculcate in him. In other words, learning is not compartmentalized in one area of life, but it must continually permeate the whole of existence.

In Proverbs 4:23 the heart [lēb] is used again to speak of the centre of the person that controls the rational and emotional life. Farmer (1991: 40) summarizes the significance of lēb in this context:

> The Hebrew word leb/lebab (translated 'heart') can also be translated 'mind' because its range of meaning in Hebrew includes concepts we often associate with the word 'mind' in English. The 'heart/mind' represents the place within the human body where both rational and emotional decisions are made. In vv. 23–27 the instructor's advice encompasses the heart (v. 23), the mouth and lips (v. 24), the eyes (v. 25), and the feet (vv.

---

[6] Whybray (1994b: 61) observes: '. . . in Dt. 6:8; 11:18 it is enjoined on the Israelites that they should bind Yahweh's words on their hands and foreheads. This was probably intended as a metaphor for keeping them constantly in mind, though later Judaism took it literally in the custom of wearing phylacteries. Whether there is an echo of Deuteronomy here or whether this was simply a current metaphor like that in the following line is not clear.'

26–27). Each part named represents an activity which ought to be governed by wisdom teachings. Only a concerted effort by the whole person can succeed at wisdom's task.

The heart is the 'wellspring of life', so it must be guarded more than anything else (Whybray 1994b: 82). Control of this vital centre of personal existence comes by choice, not by chance, for the learner is exhorted, 'guard your heart'. The learner is personally responsible to decide to keep his heart aligned to wisdom. When the heart, from which all of life springs, is guarded, then all subsidiary areas of the person, including hearing (4:20–22), speech (4:24), sight (4:25) and action (4:26–27), are affected. The ultimate result is that the learner stays on the path of wisdom, without swerving to the right or to the left.

The integrating point for the learner's life must be the fear of Yahweh, the fundamental concept which is the foundation (*cf.* pages 35–39) and the goal (*cf.* pages 84–85) for wisdom in Proverbs 1 – 9. It is the fear of Yahweh that is the primary principle of knowledge (1:7) and wisdom (9:10). By contrast, folly refuses to choose the fear of Yahweh (1:29). As Aitken (1986: 15) remarks, this concept 'touches the pulse of Israel's religious faith and practice in all its vitality, embracing reverence for and devotion to God, and, above all, loyalty and obedience to him.' In order to assimilate wisdom, the learner must organize all of life according to the fear of Yahweh. This commitment integrates every aspect of personal existence into a coherent philosophy of life predicated on wisdom.

Conclusion

In Proverbs 1 – 9 both the teacher and the learner bear responsibility for the success of the pedagogical experience. The role of the learner is to receive wisdom by listening attentively to instruction. The learner also must respond with obedience to the direction he has received from his teacher. In addition, the learner must value wisdom by embracing the way of Yahweh, rather than placing confidence in his own understanding. Furthermore, the learner must assimilate wisdom as the central principle that organizes a coherent philosophy of life around the fear of Yahweh.

This crucial role of the learner is implied in the concluding juxtaposition of parallel invitations in Proverbs 9:1–6 and 13–18.[7] Both wisdom and folly call for the learner's attention, obedience, love and commitment. The alternatives are mutually exclusive. In the final analysis, it is the learner alone who must choose which invitation he will accept. The choice that the learner makes will determine the course and consequences of his life.

---

[7] Whybray (1994b: 140) notes the significance of Proverbs 9 within the structure of Proverbs 1 – 9: 'This chapter – apart from vv. 7–12 – makes an impressive conclusion to chapters 1 – 9. The choice between wisdom and folly frequently set out in both the preceding Instructions and the two speeches by Wisdom in chapters 1 and 8 is now presented in two contrasting vignettes (vv. 1–6, 13–18) whose effectiveness is created by the close similarity between the scenes portrayed up to the final devastating conclusion: those who accept Wisdom's invitation will receive the gift of life (v. 6); those who accept that of the woman Folly will join her other guests in death (v. 18).'

Conclusion

Retrospect

The goal of this monograph has been to synthesize the data of Proverbs 1 – 9 into a systematic statement of the implicit pedagogical theory that underlies its teachings. By analysing the language and form of the biblical text, and organizing the material into the standard categories of pedagogy, this study has reconstructed the implicit view of education embedded in this prominent portion of the biblical wisdom corpus.

The worldview of Proverbs 1 – 9 (chapter 1) comprises several key assumptions that shaped the concept of education. The universe is the creation of Yahweh, the sole God. All of the universe is consequently dependent upon Yahweh for its origin and its continued existence. Yahweh as sovereign orders the world which he created, so there is a significant degree of predictability between acts and consequences. Because Yahweh is a moral governor of the universe, the world is knowable to a great degree, but his transcendence means that he has chosen to leave some of life inscrutable to humans. The fundamental responsibility for humans living in Yahweh's world is to reverence him in their lives.

The worldview of wisdom shapes the *values for education* that Proverbs 1 – 9 espouses (chapter 2). The key value championed in this text is wisdom, skill in living within the moral order of Yahweh's world. In addition, Proverbs 1 – 9 praises the values of teachability, righteousness and genuine life. Each of these values is taught both positively and in antithesis to counterfeit alternatives.

Proverbs 1 – 9 contains numerous explicit and implicit indicators of the *goals for education* (chapter 3). Although knowledge is not unimportant, the most prominent goals build upon knowledge to cultivate the learner as a mature, godly person. Pedagogy, therefore, focuses its attention on developing the learner's commitment, character and competence. Moreover, wisdom endeavours to provide for the learner protection and prosperity. The ultimate goal for education is that the learner may achieve the knowledge of God.

The *curriculum for education* in Proverbs 1 – 9 denotes the base of knowledge communicated through instruction (chapter 4). The full range of experience in Yahweh's world is the textbook for wisdom, including observation of the physical environment and human behaviour, tradition mediated through the teacher, and immediate revelation from Yahweh. Although multiple sources of truth are acknowledged, there is a basic unity of truth finding its ultimate source in the omniscience of Yahweh.

Proverbs 1 – 9 employs a wide variety of rhetorical techniques as strategies for *the process of instruction* (chapter 5). The sayings in this section are at times highly directive, but on occasion focus almost exclusively on learner involvement. For the most part, however, the teacher gives commands combined with some type of logical substantiation in order to persuade the learner to choose for himself the wise direction.

The *role of the teacher* (chapter 6) can be discerned through the rhetorical strategies he uses. Instances of highly directive language suggest that the teacher is the expert authority who actively directs the learning process. When the learner is placed at the centre of the pedagogical situation, then the teacher functions as a facilitator who creates conditions conducive to the learner's independent growth. Neither of these models alone is adequate to define the role of the teacher. The multifaceted role of the teacher is best described as that of a guide, who provides a high degree of direction when the learner is a novice, but then gradually becomes more of an enabler to assist the learner toward independent competence.

The *role of the learner* is also crucial in the accomplishment of a successful educational experience (chapter 7). The learner must receive wisdom, respond with obedience to the direction he receives, value the way of wisdom rather than choosing his own course of life, and assimilate wisdom as the integrating point of his entire life.

Prospect

This monograph has been a descriptive synthesis that has endeavoured to define the implicit pedagogical theory in Proverbs 1 – 9. The study can stand on its own as a valid object of enquiry. In doing so it remedies in part the scant prior attention given to the issues of pedagogy in Proverbs 1 – 9 (Fox 1994: 233–234).

At the same time, it also raises related questions that merit further investigation. These issues may be grouped into several general categories. In terms of biblical theology, one is prompted to ask, How did the pedagogical theory of Proverbs 1 – 9 fit into the larger corpus of biblical wisdom? It would be useful to apply the approach employed in this study to Proverbs 10 – 31, in order to establish, if possible, a comprehensive pedagogical theory for the whole canonical document. Widening the range of investigation even more, similar studies of Ecclesiastes and Job could analyse whether both practical and speculative biblical wisdom are fundamentally part of a larger unity of wisdom thought. In other words, is it possible to reconstruct a pedagogical theory which adequately encompasses all of the biblical wisdom tradition? Another avenue for research would be a comparison between the implicit pedagogical theory of the wisdom tradition and the legal, prophetic and hymnic traditions of the Hebrew Bible. To what extent is there a demonstrably consistent conception of education in the biblical texts of ancient Israel?

A second group of issues raised by this study centres on the history of interpretation. For example, how did the extrabiblical wisdom texts (*e.g.* Wisdom of Solomon and Ecclesiasticus) adopt and adapt the pedagogical theory of Proverbs 1 – 9? In addition, how does New Testament and early Christian paraenesis reflect and revise what has been described in Proverbs 1 – 9?

Thirdly, questions of application focus on the legitimacy of using the model of pedagogy suggested by Proverbs 1 – 9 in contexts that are different from the original setting in ancient Israel. To what extent can the pedagogical theory of Proverbs 1 – 9 be contextualized in the contemporary world? Can one with validity elevate its content from description to prescription? If so, then how could the theory intimated in Proverbs 1 – 9 find appropriate concrete expression in educational contexts today?

A final set of questions revolves around issues of integration between the biblical data of Proverbs 1 – 9 and the vast resource of human thought concerning pedagogy. For instance, one could compare the implicit pedagogical theory of Proverbs 1 – 9 with the explicit pedagogical models of key figures such as Plato, Rousseau, Dewey and Piaget. A more targeted approach could view a single area of pedagogy, such as the role of the teacher, and integrate what Proverbs 1 – 9 suggests with a wide range of alternatives in the academic literature.

This monograph was designed to fill a demonstrated gap in knowledge. In attempting to accomplish that goal, however, fresh questions have emerged, which demand additional research and reflection. Although the present study focuses upon the description of the educational model embedded in Proverbs 1 – 9, it does at times broach the wider questions that this text raises in the areas of biblical theology, the history of interpretation, application and integration. Much work, therefore, remains to be done in expounding the relationship between biblical wisdom and pedagogy.

Bibliography

Ahlström, G. W. (1979), 'The House of Wisdom', *Svensk Exegetisk Arsbok* 44: 74–76.

Aitken, K. T. (1986), *Proverbs*, The Daily Study Bible, Philadelphia: Westminster.

Albright, W. F. (1955), 'Some Canaanite-Phoenician Sources of Hebrew Wisdom', VTSupp 3: 1–15.

Alden, R. L. (1983), *Proverbs*, Grand Rapids: Baker.

Barré, M. L. (1981), ' "Fear of God" and the World View of Wisdom', *BTB* 11.2: 41–43.

Barucq, A. (1964), *Le Livre des Proverbs*, Sources Bibliques, Paris: Gabalda.

Bergant, D. (1984), *What are they Saying about Wisdom Literature?*, New York: Paulist.

Bergman, J. (1978), *TDOT* III: 271–272.

Blank, S. H. (1962a), 'Proverbs, Book of', *IDB* III: 936–940, Nashville/New York: Abingdon.

——(1962b), 'Wisdom', *IDB* IV: 852–861, Nashville/New York: Abingdon.

Blenkinsopp, J. (1983), *Wisdom and Law in the Old Testament*, The Oxford Bible Series, Oxford: Oxford University Press.

——(1991), 'The Social Context of the "Outsider Woman" in Proverbs 1 – 9', *Biblica* 72: 457–473.

Blocher, H. (1977), 'The Fear of the Lord as the "Principle" of Wisdom', *TynB* 28: 3–28.

Bloom, B. S. *et al.* (1956), *Taxonomy of Educational Objectives* (New York: David McKay).

Bloomfield, M. W. (1984), 'The Tradition and Style of Biblical Wisdom Literature', in D. H. Hirsch and N. Aschkenasy (eds.), *Biblical Patterns in Modern Literature*, 19–30, Brown Judaic Studies 77, Chico: Scholars Press.

Boström, L. (1990), *The God of the Sages*, Coniectanea Biblical Old Testament Series 29, Stockholm: Almqvist and Wiksell.

Brongers, H. A. (1948), 'La Crainte du Seigneur', *OTS* 5: 151–173.

Brueggemann, W. (1972), *In Man We Trust*, Richmond: John Knox.

Bullock, C. H. (1979), *An Introduction to the Old Testament Poetic Books*, Chicago: Moody.

Camp, C. V. (1985), *Wisdom and the Feminine in the Book of Proverbs*, Bible and Literature Series 11, Sheffield: Almond.

——(1991), 'What's so Strange about the Strange Woman?', in D. Jobling *et al.* (eds.), *The Bible and the Politics of Exegesis*, 17–31, Cleveland: Pilgrim.

Childs, B. S. (1979), *Introduction to the Old Testament as Scripture*, Philadelphia: Fortress.

Cleife, D. H. (1976), 'Authority', in D. I. Lloyd (ed.), *Philosophy and the Teacher*, 128–137, London: Routledge and Kegan Paul.

Clements, R. E. (1988), 'Solomon and the Origins of Wisdom in Israel', *Perspectives in Religious Studies* 15: 23–35.

——(1990), *Wisdom for a Changing World: Wisdom in Old Testament Theology*, Berkeley Lectures 2, Berkeley, CA: Bibal.

——(1992), *Wisdom in Theology*, Grand Rapids: Eerdmans.

——(1993), 'The Good Neighbor in the Book of Proverbs', in H. A. McKay and D. J. A. Clines (eds.), *Of Prophets' Visions and the Wisdom of Sages*, JSOTSupp 162: 209–228, Sheffield: JSOT.

——(1995), 'Wisdom and Old Testament Theology', in J. Day *et al.* (eds.), *Wisdom in Ancient Israel*, 269–286, Cambridge: Cambridge University Press.

Clifford, R. J. (1993), 'Woman Wisdom in the Book of Proverbs', in G. Braulik *et al.* (eds.), *Biblische Theologie und Gesellschaftlicher Wandel*, 61–72, Freiburg, Herder.

Cohen, A. (1952), *Proverbs*, The Soncino Books of the Bible, London: Soncino.

Collins, J. J. (1980a), 'Proverbial Wisdom and the Yahwist Vision', *Semeia* 17: 1–17.

——(1980b), *Proverbs, Ecclesiastes*, Knox Preaching Guides, Atlanta: John Knox.

Combs, A. W. (1982), *A Personal Approach to Teaching*, Boston: Allyn and Bacon.

Cox, D. (1982a) 'Fear or Conscience? *yir'at YHWH* in Proverbs 1 – 9', *Studia Hierosolymitana* 3: 83–90.

——(1982b), *Proverbs with an Introduction to Sapiential Books*, Old Testament Message 17, Wilmington, DE: Michael Glazier.

——(1987), 'Learning and the Way to God', *Studia Missionalia* 36: 1–23.

——(1990) 'Human Dignity in Old Testament Wisdom', *Studia Missionalia* 39: 1–19.

——(1993), 'The New Writers: Wisdom's Response to a Changing Society', *Studia Missionalia* 42: 1–15.

Craigie, P. C. (1979), 'Biblical Wisdom in the Modern World: I. Proverbs', *Crux* 15.4: 7–9.

Crenshaw, J. L. (1969), 'Method in Determining Wisdom Influence upon "Historical" Literature', *JBL* 88: 129–142.

——(1974), 'Wisdom', in J. H. Hayes (ed.), *Old Testament Form Criticism*, 225–264, San Antonio: Trinity University Press.

——(1977), 'In Search of Divine Presence: Some Remarks Preliminary to a Theology of Wisdom', *Review and Expositor* 74: 353–369.

——(1980), 'Impossible Questions, Sayings, and Tasks', *Semeia* 17: 19–34.

——(1981a), *Old Testament Wisdom*, Atlanta: John Knox.

——(1981b), 'Wisdom and Authority: Sapiential Rhetoric and its Warrants', VTSupp 32: 10–29.

——(1985), 'Education in Ancient Israel', *JBL* 104.4: 601–615.

——(1987), 'The Acquisition of Knowledge in Israelite Wisdom Literature', *Word and World* 7: 245–252.

——(1990), 'The Sage in Proverbs', in J. G. Gammie and L. G. Perdue (eds.), *The Sage in Israel and the Ancient Near East*, 205–216, Winona Lake, IN: Eisenbrauns.

——(1993a), 'The Concept of God in Old Testament Wisdom', in L. G. Perdue et al. (eds.), *In Search of Wisdom*, 1–18, Louisville: Westminster/John Knox.

——(1993b), 'Wisdom Literature: Retrospect and Prospect', in H. A. McKay and D. J. A. Clines (eds.), *Of Prophets' Visions and the Wisdom of Sages*, JSOTSupp 162: 160–187, Sheffield: JSOT.

Curtis, E. M. (1986), 'Old Testament Wisdom: A Model for Faith-learning Integration', *Christian Scholars Review* 15.3: 213–227.

Dahood, M. (1973), 'Honey that Drips: Notes on Proverbs 5, 2–3', *Biblica* 54: 65–66.

Davidson, R. (1990), *Wisdom and Worship*, London: SCM.

Day, J., R. P. Gordon and H. G. M. Williamson (eds.) (1995), *Wisdom in Ancient Israel: Essays in Honour of J. A. Emerton* (Cambridge: Cambridge University Press).

Delitzsch, F. (1971), *The Book of Proverbs*, Commentary on the Old Testament, ET Grand Rapids: Eerdmans (German original 1872).

Derousseaux, L. (1970), *La Crainte de Dieu dans l'Ancien Testament*, Paris: Cerf.

Dewey, J. (1938), *Experience and Education*, New York: Macmillan.

——(1943), *The Child and the Curriculum*, Chicago: University of Chicago.

Duhaime, J.-L. (1980), 'Perception de Dieu et comportment moral chez les sages d'Israël', *Science et Esprit* 32.2: 193–197.

Duty, R. W. (1987), 'Creation, History, and the Ethics of the Book of Proverbs', *Word and World* 7.3: 261–271.

Eaton, J. (1989), *The Contemplative Face of Old Testament Wisdom*, London: SCM.

——(1993), 'Memory and Encounter: An Educational Ideal', in H. A. McKay and D. J. A. Clines (eds.), *Of Prophets' Visions and the Wisdom of Sages*, JSOTSupp 162: 179–191, Sheffield: JSOT.

Emerton, J. A. (1979a), 'A Note on Proverbs II.18', *JTS* NS 30.1: 153–158.

——(1979b), 'Wisdom', in G. W. Anderson (ed.), *Tradition and Interpretation*, 214–237, Oxford: Oxford University Press.

Farmer, K. A. (1991), *Who Knows What is Good?* International Theological Commentary, Grand Rapids: Eerdmans.

Fontaine, C. R. (1984), 'Brightening up the Mindworks: Concepts of Instruction in Biblical Wisdom and Rinzai Zen', *Religious Education* 79.4: 590–600.

——(1993), 'Wisdom in Proverbs', in L. G. Perdue *et al.* (eds.), *In Search of Wisdom*, 99–114, Louisville: Westminster/John Knox.

Fox, M. V. (1968), 'Aspects of the Religion of the Book of Proverbs', *HUCA* 39: 55–69.

——(1986), 'Egyptian Onomastica and Biblical Wisdom', *VT* 36.3: 302–310.

——(1994), 'The Pedagogy of Proverbs 2', *JBL* 113: 233–243.

——(1996), ''Amon again', *JBL* 115: 699–702.

Fuhs, H. F. (1990), *TDOT* VI: 290–315.

Garrett, D. A. (1990), 'Votive Prostitution Again: A Comparison of Proverbs 7:13–14 and 21:28–29', *JBL* 109: 681–682.

——(1993), *Proverbs, Ecclesiastes, Song of Songs*, The New American Commentary 14, Nashville: Broadman.

Gemser, B. (1953), 'The Importance of the Motive Clause in Old

Testament Law', VTSupp 1: 50–66.

Giese, R. L. (1992), 'Strength through Wisdom and the Bee in LXX Prov 6, 8a–c', *Biblica* 73: 404–411.

——(1993), 'Dualism in the LXX of Prov 2:17: A Case Study in the LXX as Revisionary Translation', *JETS* 36: 289–295.

Goldingay, J. E. (1977), 'Proverbs V and IX', *Revue Biblique* 84: 80–93.

——(1979), 'The "Salvation History" Perspective and the "Wisdom Perspective" within the Context of Biblical Theology', *EQ* 51: 194–207.

Greenstone, J. (1950), *Proverbs*, Philadelphia: Jewish Publication Society.

Gronlund, N. E. (1985), *Stating Objectives for Classroom Instruction*, 3rd edn, New York: Macmillan (1st edn 1970).

Habel, N. C. (1972), 'The Symbolism of Wisdom in Proverbs 1 – 9', *Int* 26: 131–157.

Hadley, J. M. (1995), 'Wisdom and the Goddess', in J. Day *et al.* (eds.), *Wisdom in Ancient Israel*, 234–243, Cambridge: Cambridge University Press.

Healey, J. F. (1989), 'Models of Behavior: Matt 6:26 (// Luke 12:24) and Prov 6:6–8', *JBL* 108: 497–498.

Heck, S. F. and C. R. Williams (1984), *The Complex Roles of the Teacher: An Ecological Perspective*, New York: Teachers College Press.

Hensell, E. (1981), 'The "Proverbial" in Proverbs', *The Bible Today* 19.3: 162–167.

Hermisson, H.-J. (1984), 'Observations on the Creation Theology in Wisdom', in B. W. Anderson (ed.), *Creation in the Old Testament*, Issues in Religion and Theology 6: 118–134, Philadelphia: Fortress.

Holmes, A. F. (1983), *Contours of a World View*, Grand Rapids: Eerdmans, and Leicester: Inter-Varsity Press.

Hoppe, L. J. (1981), 'The Words of the Wise, *The Bible Today* 19.3: 155–161.

Hubbard, D. A. (1966), 'The Wisdom Movement and Israel's Covenant Faith', *TynB* 17: 3–33.

——(1989), *Proverbs*, The Communicator's Commentary 15a, Dallas: Word Books.

Hyman, R. T. (1970), *Ways of Teaching*, Philadelphia: J. B. Lippincott.

Irwin, W. A. (1961), 'Where shall Wisdom be Found?', *JBL* 80: 133–142.

Jenks, A. W. (1985), 'Theological Presuppositions of Israel's Wisdom Literature', *Horizons in Biblical Theology* 7.1: 43–75.

Johnson, J. E. (1987), 'An Analysis of Proverbs 1:1–7', *Bibliotheca Sacra* 144. 576: 419–432.

Johnson, P. E. (1995), *Reason in the Balance*, Downers Grove, IL: InterVarsity.

Kayatz, C. (1966), *Studien zu Proverbien 1 – 9*, Neukirchen-Vluyn: Neukircher.

Kidner, D. (1984), *The Proverbs*, Tyndale Old Testament Commentaries, Leicester and Downers Grove, IL: Inter-Varsity Press.

Kitchen, K. A. (1977), 'Proverbs and Wisdom Books of the Ancient Near East', *TynB* 28: 69–114.

Koch, K. (1978), *TDOT* III: 271–272.

Krathwohl, D. R. *et al.* (1964), *Taxonomy of Educational Objectives: Handbook II, Affective Domain*, New York: David McKay.

Kruger, P. A. (1987), 'Promiscuity or Marriage Fidelity? A Note on Prov 5:15–18', *JNSL* 13: 61–68.

Landes, G. M. (1974), 'Creation Tradition in Proverbs 8:22–31 and Genesis 1', in H. N. Bream *et al.* (eds.), *A Light Unto My Path*, Gettysburg Theological Studies 4: 279–292, Philadelphia: Temple University Press.

Lang, B. (1986), *Wisdom and the Book of Proverbs*, New York: Pilgrim.

McKane, W. (1970), *Proverbs*, The Old Testament Library, Philadelphia: Westminster.

McKenzie, J. L. (1967), 'Reflections on Wisdom', *JBL* 86: 1–9.

Malchow, B. V. (1982), 'Social Justice in the Wisdom Literature', *BTB* 12.4: 120–124.

——(1983), 'Wisdom's Contribution to Dialogue', *BTB* 13.4: 111–115.

Marsden, G. M. (1994), *The Soul of the American University*, New York: Oxford University Press.

Matlack, H. (1988), 'The Play of Wisdom', *Currents in Theology and Mission* 15.5: 425–430.

Meinhold, A. (1991), *Die Sprüche. Teil 1: Sprüche Kapitel 1 – 15*, Zürcher Bibelkommentaire Altes Testament 16.1, Zürich: Theologischer.

Melchert, C. F. (1990), 'Creation and Justice among the Sages',

Religious Education 85: 368–381.

——(1992), 'Wisdom is Vindicated by Her Deeds', *Religious Education* 87: 127–151.

Morgan, D. F. (1994), 'Searching for Biblical Wisdom', *Sewanee Theological Review* 37: 151–162.

Mouser, W. E. (1983), *Walking in Wisdom: Studying the Proverbs of Solomon*, Downers Grove, IL: InterVarsity.

Murphy, R. E. (1966), 'The Kerygma of the Book of Proverbs', *Int* 20: 3–14.

——(1969), 'The Interpretation of Old Testament Wisdom Literature', *Int* 23: 289–301.

——(1970), 'The Hebrew Sage and Openness to the World', in J. Papin (ed.), *Christian Action and Openness to the World*, 219–244, Villanova, PA: Villanova University Press.

——(1976), 'Wisdom Theses', in J. Armenti (ed.), *Wisdom and Knowledge*, 187–200, Villanova, PA: Villanova University Press.

——(1981a), 'Hebrew Wisdom', *JAOS* 101: 21–34.

——(1981b), 'Israel's Wisdom: A Biblical Model of Salvation', *Studia Missionalia* 30: 1–43.

——(1981c), *Wisdom Literature: Job, Proverbs, Ruth, Chronicles, Ecclesiastes, and Esther*, The Forms of the Old Testament Literature 13, Grand Rapids: Eerdmans.

——(1983), *Wisdom Literature and Psalms*, Interpreting Biblical Texts, Nashville: Abingdon.

——(1984), 'The Theological Contributions of Israel's Wisdom Literature', *Listening* 19.1: 30–40.

——(1985), 'Wisdom and Creation', *JBL* 104: 3–11.

——(1986), 'Wisdom's Song: Proverbs 1:20–33', *CBQ* 48.3: 456–460.

——(1988), 'Wisdom and Eros in Proverbs 1 – 9', *CBQ* 50.4: 600–603.

——(1990), *The Tree of Life*, The Anchor Bible Reference Library, New York: Doubleday.

Nel, P. J. (1978), 'A Proposed Method for Determining the Context of the Wisdom Admonitions', *JNSL* 6: 33–40.

——(1981a), 'Authority in the Wisdom Admonitions', *ZAW* 93.3: 418–426.

——(1981b), 'The Genres of Biblical Wisdom Literature', *JNSL* 9: 129–142.

——(1982), *The Structure and Ethos of the Wisdom Admonitions in Proverbs*, BZAW 158, Berlin/New York: Walter de Gruyter.

Newsom, C. A. (1989), 'Woman and the Discourse of Patriarchal Wisdom', in P. L. Day (ed.), *Gender and Difference in Ancient Israel*, 142–160, Minneapolis: Fortress.

Noth, M. and D. W. Thomas (eds.) (1955), *Wisdom in Israel and in the Ancient Near East*, VTSupp 3, Leiden: Brill.

Ober, R. L. *et al.* (1971), *Systematic Observation of Teaching*, Englewood Cliffs, NJ: Prentice-Hall.

O'Connell, R. H. (1991), 'Proverbs VII 16–17: A Case of Fatal Deception in a "Woman and the Window" Type-scene', *VT* 41: 235–241.

O'Conner, K. M. (1988), *The Wisdom Literature*, Message of Biblical Spirituality 5, Wilmington, DE: Michael Glazier.

Oesterley, W. O. E. (1929), *The Book of Proverbs*, Westminster Commentaries Revised, London: Methuen and Company.

Passmore, J. (1980), *The Philosophy of Teaching*, Cambridge: Harvard University Press.

Peels, H. G. L. (1994), 'Passion or Justice? The Interpretation of *Bᵉ YÔM NĀQĀM* in Proverbs VI 34', *VT* 44: 270–274.

Perdue, L. G. (1977), *Wisdom and Cult*, SBLDS 30, Missoula: Scholars Press.

——(1981), 'Liminality as a Social Setting for Wisdom Instructions', *ZAW* 93.1: 114–126.

——(1990), 'Cosmology and the Social Order in the Wisdom Tradition', in J. G. Gammie and L. G. Perdue (eds.), *The Sage in Israel and the Ancient Near East*, 457–478, Winona Lake, IN: Eisenbrauns.

——(1993), 'Wisdom in the Book of Job', in L. G. Perdue *et al.* (eds.), *In Search of Wisdom*, Louisville: Westminster/John Knox.

——(1994), *Wisdom and Creation*, Nashville: Abingdon.

Plaut, W. G. (1961), *Book of Proverbs*, The Jewish Commentary for Bible Readers, New York: Union of American Hebrew Congregations.

Pleins, J. D. (1987), 'Poverty in the Social World of the Wise', *JSOT* 37: 61–78.

Rad, G. von (1962, 1965), *Old Testament Theology*, 2 vols, New York: Harper and Row.

——(1972), *Wisdom in Israel*, Nashville: Abingdon.

Ross, A. P. (1991), 'Proverbs', in F. E. Gaebelein (ed.), *The Expositor's Bible Commentary*, V: 881–1134, Grand Rapids: Zondervan.

Rylaarsdam, J. C. (1964), *The Proverbs, Ecclesiastes, The Song of*

Solomon, The Layman's Bible Commentary 10, Richmond: John Knox.

Scheffler, I. (1960), *The Language of Education*, Springfield, IL: Charles C. Thomas.

Scobie, C. H. H. (1984), 'The Place of Wisdom in Biblical Thinking', *BTB* 14.2: 43–48.

Scott, R. B. Y. (1955), 'Solomon and the Beginnings of Wisdom in Israel', VTSupp 3: 262–279.

——(1961), 'Priesthood, Prophecy, Wisdom, and the Knowledge of God', *JBL* 80: 1–15.

——(1965), *Proverbs, Ecclesiastes*, The Anchor Bible 18, Garden City: Doubleday and Co.

——(1971), *The Way of Wisdom in the Old Testament*, New York: Macmillan.

——(1972), 'Wise and Foolish, Righteous and Wicked', VTSupp 23: 146–165.

Shupak, N. (1993), *Where Can Wisdom Be Found?* Orbis Biblicus et Orientalis 130, Fribourg: University; Gottingen: Vandenhoeck and Ruprecht.

Sire, J. W. (1988), *The Universe Next Door*, 2nd edn, Leicester and Downers Grove, IL: Inter-Varsity Press (1st edn 1976).

Skehan, P. W. (1979), 'Structures in Poems on Wisdom', *CBQ* 41: 365–379.

Targum of Proverbs (1991), in The Aramaic Bible 15, Collegeville, MN: Liturgical Press.

Toombs, L. E. (1955), 'OT Theology and the Wisdom Literature', *JBR* 23: 193–196.

——(1988), 'The Theology and Ethics of the Book of Proverbs', *Consensus* 14.2: 7–24.

Toy, C. C. (1902), *A Critical and Exegetical Commentary on the Book of Proverbs*, International Critical Commentary, New York: Charles Scribner's Sons.

Van Leeuwen, R. C. (1990), 'Liminality and Worldview in Proverbs 1 – 9', *Semeia* 50: 111–144.

——(1992), 'Wealth and Poverty: System and Contradiction in Proverbs', *Hebrew Studies* 33: 25–36.

Vawter, B. (1972), 'Intimations of Immortality and the Old Testament', *JBL* 92: 158–171.

——(1980), 'Prov 8:22: Wisdom and Creation', *JBL* 99: 205–216.

——(1986), 'Yahweh: Lord of the Heavens and the Earth', *CBQ* 48.3: 461–467.

Walsh, B. J. and J. R. Middleton (1984), *The Transforming Vision*, Downers Grove, IL: InterVarsity.

Waltke, B. K. (1979a), 'The Book of Proverbs and Ancient Wisdom Literature', *Bibliotheca Sacra* 136.543: 221–238.

——(1979b), 'The Book of Proverbs and Old Testament Theology', *Bibliotheca Sacra* 136.544: 302–317.

——(1987), 'The Authority of Proverbs: An Exposition of Proverbs 1:2–6', *Presbyterian* 13.2: 65–78.

Walton, J. H. (1989), *Ancient Israelite Literature in its Cultural Context*, Library of Biblical Interpretation, Grand Rapids: Zondervan.

Westermann, C. (1995), *Roots of Wisdom*, Louisville: Westminster/John Knox.

Whybray, R. N. (1965), *Wisdom in Proverbs: The Concept of Wisdom in Proverbs 1 – 9*, Studies in Biblical Theology, London: SCM.

——(1972), *The Book of Proverbs*, The Cambridge Bible Commentary, Cambridge: Cambridge University Press.

——(1974), *The Intellectual Tradition in the Old Testament*, BZAW 135, Berlin/New York: Walter de Gruyter.

——(1994a), *The Composition of the Book of Proverbs*, JSOTSupp 168, Sheffield: JSOT.

——(1994b), *Proverbs*, The New Century Bible Commentary, Grand Rapids: Eerdmans.

Williams, D. H. (1994), 'Proverbs 8:22–31', *Int* 48: 275–279.

Williams, J. G. (1981), *Those Who Ponder Proverbs: Aphoristic Thinking and Biblical Literature*, Bible and Literature Series, Sheffield: Almond.

Wilson, F. M. (1987), 'Sacred and Profane? The Yahwistic Redaction of Proverbs Reconsidered', in K. G. Hoglund *et al.* (eds.), *The Listening Heart*, JSOTSupp 58: 313–334, Sheffield: Sheffield Academic Press.

Wilson, G. H. (1984), ' "The Words of the Wise": The Intent and Significance of Qohelet 12:9–14', *JBL* 103.2: 175–182.

Yee, G. A. (1989), ' "I have perfumed my bed with myrrh": The Foreign Woman (*'iššâ zārâ*) in Proverbs 1 – 9', *JSOT* 43: 53–68.

——(1992), 'The Theology of Creation in Proverbs 8:22–23', in R. J. Clifford and J. J. Collins (eds.), *Creation in the Biblical Traditions*, CBQMS 24: 85–96, Washington: Catholic Biblical Association.

Zornberg, A. G. (1982), *Malbim on Mishley: The Commentary of*

Rabbi Meir Leibush Malbim on the Book of Proverbs, Jerusalem: Feldheim.

Zuck, R. B. (ed.) (1995), *Learning from the Sages: Selected Studies on the Book of Proverbs*, Grand Rapids: Baker.

Index of Scripture references

168

Index of authors

Aitken, K. 24, 31, 36n, 44, 45, 46n,
48, 56, 65, 66, 71, 74, 76, 78, 78n,
80, 81n, 82, 92, 94, 113n, 114,
114n, 118, 121, 122n, 139, 141,
142n, 144, 148
Alden, R. 23, 54, 120

Barré, M. 26, 37
Barucq, A. 82
Bergant, D. 34n
Bergman, J. 113n
Blank, S. 43n
Blenkinsopp, J. 55, 79n, 122n
Blocher, H. 35n, 36
Bloom, B. 63n
Bloomfield, M. 31n, 32
Bostrom, L. 16, 23, 24, 29, 33n, 88,
119n
Brongers, H. 35n, 38
Brueggemann, W. 26, 37, 129n

Camp, C. 79n
Childs, B. 17, 64
Cleife, D. 126
Clements, R. 22, 23, 24n, 37, 38,
68, 83, 92, 93n
Clifford, R. 123n
Cohen, A. 24, 30n, 32, 36, 46, 51,
52n, 54, 66, 80, 114, 120, 142n
Collins, J. 58
Combs, A. 128, 129, 131
Cox, D. 15, 30, 35n, 48, 83, 90, 96,
104, 138
Craigie, P. 21, 36, 69, 87, 102n
Crenshaw, J. 22, 30, 36, 41, 47, 64,
87n, 88, 89n, 92, 93, 94n, 101,

105, 116, 120

Day, J. 18n
Delitzsch, F. 24, 70
Derousseaux, L. 35n
Dewey, J. 130, 131, 133n, 154
Dilthey, W. 19
Duhaime, J. 28, 70

Eaton, J. 22, 28, 67, 116, 133, 144
Emerton, J. 28

Farmer, K. 24n, 30, 46, 54, 56n, 57,
69, 85, 92n, 147
Fox, M. 17, 18, 24n, 28, 63, 68, 71,
74n, 119, 153
Fuhs, H. 35n

Garrett, D. 24, 59, 91n, 116, 138n
Goldingay, J. 96
Gordon, R. 18n
Greenstone, J. 56n, 59, 65, 72, 73,
85, 96, 146
Gronlund, N. 63n, 135, 136, 140,
144, 147

Habel, N. 113
Hadley, J. 79n
Heck, S. 129, 131
Holmes, A. 19, 25, 30
Hoppe, L. 83
Hubbard, D. 33, 38, 64
Hyman, R. 129n

Johnson, P. 129